MW00795728

NKJV

LUKE-ACTS DEVOTIONAL

FLIPBACK

NKJV
LUKE-ACTS DEVOTIONAL
FLIPBACK

52 Devotional Guides on Jesus' Life
and the Church

THOMAS NELSON
Since 1798

www.ThomasNelson.com

NKJV Luke-Acts Devotional Flipback Edition
Copyright © 2022 by Thomas Nelson
Published in Nashville, Tennessee, by Thomas Nelson.
Thomas Nelson is a registered trademark of HarperCollins Christian Publishing, Inc.

Holy Bible, New King James Version®
Copyright © 1982 by Thomas Nelson
All rights reserved.

Library of Congress Control Number: 2022932386

This Bible was set in the Thomas Nelson NKJV Typeface, created at the 2K/DENMARK
type foundry.

Printed in the Netherlands

22 23 24 25 26 27 28 /RJN/ 15 14 13 12 11 10 9 8 7 6 5 4 3 2 1

CONTENTS

PREFACE TO THE
NEW KING JAMES VERSION®

To understand the heart behind the New King James Version, one need look no further than the stated intentions of the original King James scholars: "Not to make a new translation . . . but to make a good one better." The New King James Version is a continuation of the labors of the King James translators, unlocking for today's readers the spiritual treasures found especially in the Authorized Version of the Holy Bible.

While seeking to maintain the excellent *form* of the traditional English Bible, special care has also been taken to preserve the work of *precision* which is the legacy of the King James translators.

Where new translation has been necessary, the most complete representation of the original has been rendered by considering the definition and usage of the Greek words in their contexts. This translation principle, known as *complete equivalence*, seeks to preserve accurately all of the information in the text while presenting it in good literary form.

In addition to accuracy, the translators have also sought to maintain those lyrical and devotional qualities that are so highly regarded in the King James Version. The thought flow and selection of phrases from the King James Version have been preserved wherever possible without sacrificing clarity.

The format of the New King James Version is designed to enhance the vividness, devotional quality, and usefulness of the Bible. Words or phrases in italics indicate expressions in the original language that require clarification by additional English words, as was done in the King James Version. The covenant name of God was usually translated from the Hebrew as Lord or God, using capital letters as shown, as in the King James Version. This convention is also maintained in the New King James Version when the Old Testament is quoted in the New.

The Greek text used for the New Testament is the one that was followed by the King James translators: the traditional text of the Greek-speaking churches, called the Received Text or Textus Receptus, first published in 1516. Footnotes indicate significant variants from the Textus Receptus as found in two other editions of the Greek New Testament:

(1) NU-Text: These variations generally represent the Alexandrian or Egyptian text type as found in the critical text published in the

twenty-seventh edition of the Nestle-Aland Greek New Testament (N) and in the United Bible Societies' third edition (U).

(2) M-Text: These variations represent readings found in the text of *The Greek New Testament According to the Majority Text*, which follows the consensus of the majority of surviving New Testament manuscripts.

The textual notes in the New King James Version make no evaluation but objectively present the facts about variant readings.

INTRODUCTION

The Gospel of Luke and The Acts of the Apostles recorded the life of Jesus and the birth of the church. This *NKJV Luke-Acts Devotional Flipback Bible* is offered as a guide for you to deepen your faith and widen your view of God's work. In the back of this edition, you will find fifty-two devotional prompts—one for each chapter of Luke and Acts. Here are a few suggestions on their use:

- Read Luke in December for the Advent season and Acts in January to begin the new year.
- Annual devotion plan: Use them to guide a year of personal Bible reading.
- Guide for family discussions: As a family, read the passage and use the prompts to spark faith-centered conversations throughout the year.

angel said to her, "Rejoice, highly favored *one*, the Lord *is* with you; blessed *are* you among women!"[a]

29But when she saw *him*,[a] she was troubled at his saying, and considered what manner of greeting this was. 30Then the angel said to her, "Do not be afraid, Mary, for you have found favor with God. 31And behold, you will conceive in your womb and bring forth a Son, and shall call His name JESUS. 32He will be great, and will be called the Son of the Highest; and the Lord God will give Him the throne of His father David. 33And He will reign over the house of Jacob forever, and of His kingdom there will be no end."

34Then Mary said to the angel, "How can this be, since I do not know a man?"

35And the angel answered and said to her, "*The* Holy Spirit will come upon you, and the power of the Highest will overshadow you; therefore, also, that Holy One who is to be born will be called the Son of God. 36Now indeed, Elizabeth your relative has also conceived a son in her old age; and this is now the sixth month for her who was called barren. 37For with God nothing will be impossible." 38Then Mary said, "Behold the maidservant of the Lord! Let it be to me according to your word." And the angel departed from her.

1:28 a NU-Text omits *blessed are you among women*.   1:29 a NU-Text omits *when she saw him*.

LUKE 1:39

MARY VISITS ELIZABETH

39 Now Mary arose in those days and went into the hill country with haste, to a city of Judah, 40 and entered the house of Zacharias and greeted Elizabeth. 41 And it happened, when Elizabeth heard the greeting of Mary, that the babe leaped in her womb; and Elizabeth was filled with the Holy Spirit. 42 Then she spoke out with a loud voice and said, "Blessed *are* you among women, and blessed *is* the fruit of your womb! 43 But why *is* this *granted* to me, that the mother of my Lord should come to me? 44 For indeed, as soon as the voice of your greeting sounded in my ears, the babe leaped in my womb for joy. 45 Blessed *is* she who believed, for there will be a fulfillment of those things which were told her from the Lord."

THE SONG OF MARY

46 And Mary said:

"My soul magnifies the Lord,
47 And my spirit has rejoiced in God my Savior.
48 For He has regarded the lowly state of His maidservant;
For behold, henceforth all generations will call me blessed.
49 For He who is mighty has done great things for me,

And holy *is* His name.
50 And His mercy *is* on those who fear Him
From generation to generation.
51 He has shown strength with His arm;
He has scattered *the* proud in the imagination of their hearts.
52 He has put down the mighty from *their* thrones,
And exalted *the* lowly.
53 He has filled *the* hungry with good things,
And *the* rich He has sent away empty.
54 He has helped His servant Israel,
In remembrance of *His* mercy,
55 As He spoke to our fathers,
To Abraham and to his seed forever."

56 And Mary remained with her about three months, and returned to her house.

BIRTH OF JOHN THE BAPTIST

57 Now Elizabeth's full time came for her to be delivered, and she brought forth a son. 58 When her neighbors and relatives heard how the Lord had shown great mercy to her, they rejoiced with her.

CIRCUMCISION OF JOHN THE BAPTIST

⁵⁹So it was, on the eighth day, that they came to circumcise the child; and they would have called him by the name of his father, Zacharias. ⁶⁰His mother answered and said, "No; he shall be called John."

⁶¹But they said to her, "There is no one among your relatives who is called by this name." ⁶²So they made signs to his father—what he would have him called.

⁶³And he asked for a writing tablet, and wrote, saying, "His name is John." So they all marveled. ⁶⁴Immediately his mouth was opened and his tongue *loosed*, and he spoke, praising God. ⁶⁵Then fear came on all who dwelt around them; and all these sayings were discussed throughout all the hill country of Judea. ⁶⁶And all those who heard *them* kept *them* in their hearts, saying, "What kind of child will this be?" And the hand of the Lord was with him.

ZACHARIAS' PROPHECY

⁶⁷Now his father Zacharias was filled with the Holy Spirit, and prophesied, saying:

⁶⁸"Blessed *is* the Lord God of Israel,
    For He has visited and redeemed His people,

69 And has raised up a horn of salvation for us
   In the house of His servant David,
70 As He spoke by the mouth of His holy prophets,
   Who *have been* since the world began,
71 That we should be saved from our enemies
   And from the hand of all who hate us,
72 To perform the mercy *promised* to our fathers
   And to remember His holy covenant,
73 The oath which He swore to our father Abraham:
74 To grant us that we,
   Being delivered from the hand of our enemies,
   Might serve Him without fear,
75 In holiness and righteousness before
   Him all the days of our life.

76 "And you, child, will be called the prophet of the Highest;
   For you will go before the face of the
   Lord to prepare His ways,
77 To give knowledge of salvation to His people
   By the remission of their sins,

78 Through the tender mercy of our God,
   With which the Dayspring from on high has visited^a us;
79 To give light to those who sit in darkness
   and the shadow of death,
   To guide our feet into the way of peace."

80 So the child grew and became strong in spirit, and was in the deserts till the day of his manifestation to Israel.

CHRIST BORN OF MARY

2 And it came to pass in those days *that* a decree went out from Caesar Augustus that all the world should be registered. 2 This census first took place while Quirinius was governing Syria. 3 So all went to be registered, everyone to his own city.

4 Joseph also went up from Galilee, out of the city of Nazareth, into Judea, to the city of David, which is called Bethlehem, because he was of the house and lineage of David, 5 to be registered with Mary, his betrothed wife,^a who was with child. 6 So it was, that while they were there, the days were completed for her to be delivered. 7 And she brought forth her firstborn Son, and wrapped Him

in swaddling cloths, and laid Him in a manger, because there was no room for them in the inn.

GLORY IN THE HIGHEST

8Now there were in the same country shepherds living out in the fields, keeping watch over their flock by night. 9And behold,[a] an angel of the Lord stood before them, and the glory of the Lord shone around them, and they were greatly afraid. 10Then the angel said to them, "Do not be afraid, for behold, I bring you good tidings of great joy which will be to all people. 11For there is born to you this day in the city of David a Savior, who is Christ the Lord. 12And this *will be* the sign to you: You will find a Babe wrapped in swaddling cloths, lying in a manger."

13And suddenly there was with the angel a multitude of the heavenly host praising God and saying:

14 "Glory to God in the highest,
   And on earth peace, goodwill toward men!"[a]

15So it was, when the angels had gone away from them into heaven, that the

1:78 [a] NU-Text reads *shall visit.* 2:5 [a] NU-Text omits *wife.* 2:9 [a] NU-Text omits *behold.*
2:14 [a] NU-Text reads *toward men of goodwill.*

LUKE 2:16

shepherds said to one another, "Let us now go to Bethlehem and see this thing that has come to pass, which the Lord has made known to us." [16]And they came with haste and found Mary and Joseph, and the Babe lying in a manger. [17]Now when they had seen *Him,* they made widely[a] known the saying which was told them concerning this Child. [18]And all those who heard *it* marveled at those things which were told them by the shepherds. [19]But Mary kept all these things and pondered *them* in her heart. [20]Then the shepherds returned, glorifying and praising God for all the things that they had heard and seen, as it was told them.

CIRCUMCISION OF JESUS

[21]And when eight days were completed for the circumcision of the Child, [a] His name was called JESUS, the name given by the angel before He was conceived in the womb.

JESUS PRESENTED IN THE TEMPLE

[22]Now when the days of her purification according to the law of Moses were completed, they brought Him to Jerusalem to present *Him* to the Lord [23](as it is written in the law of the Lord, "Every male who opens the womb shall be called

holy to the LORD"), [a] [24]and to offer a sacrifice according to what is said in the law of the Lord, "A pair of turtledoves or two young pigeons."[a]

SIMEON SEES GOD'S SALVATION

[25]And behold, there was a man in Jerusalem whose name *was* Simeon, and this man *was* just and devout, waiting for the Consolation of Israel, and the Holy Spirit was upon him. [26]And it had been revealed to him by the Holy Spirit that he would not see death before he had seen the Lord's Christ. [27]So he came by the Spirit into the temple. And when the parents brought in the Child Jesus, to do for Him according to the custom of the law, [28]he took Him up in his arms and blessed God and said:

[29] "Lord, now You are letting Your servant depart in peace,
    According to Your word;
[30] For my eyes have seen Your salvation
[31] Which You have prepared before the face of all peoples,
[32] A light to *bring* revelation to the Gentiles,
    And the glory of Your people Israel."

2:17 [a] NU-Text omits *widely.*   2:21 [a] NU-Text reads *for His circumcision.*   2:23 [a] Exodus 13:2, 12, 15
2:24 [a] Leviticus 12:8

³³And Joseph and His mother^a marveled at those things which were spoken of Him. ³⁴Then Simeon blessed them, and said to Mary His mother, "Behold, this *Child* is destined for the fall and rising of many in Israel, and for a sign which will be spoken against ³⁵(yes, a sword will pierce through your own soul also), that the thoughts of many hearts may be revealed."

ANNA BEARS WITNESS TO THE REDEEMER

³⁶Now there was one, Anna, a prophetess, the daughter of Phanuel, of the tribe of Asher. She was of a great age, and had lived with a husband seven years from her virginity; ³⁷and this woman *was* a widow of about eighty-four years,^a who did not depart from the temple, but served *God* with fastings and prayers night and day. ³⁸And coming in that instant she gave thanks to the Lord,^a and spoke of Him to all those who looked for redemption in Jerusalem.

THE FAMILY RETURNS TO NAZARETH

³⁹So when they had performed all things according to the law of the Lord, they returned to Galilee, to their *own* city, Nazareth. ⁴⁰And the Child grew and became strong in spirit,^a filled with wisdom; and the grace of God was upon Him.

THE BOY JESUS AMAZES THE SCHOLARS

41His parents went to Jerusalem every year at the Feast of the Passover. 42And when He was twelve years old, they went up to Jerusalem according to the custom of the feast. 43When they had finished the days, as they returned, the Boy Jesus lingered behind in Jerusalem. And Joseph and His mother[a] did not know it; 44but supposing Him to have been in the company, they went a day's journey, and sought Him among their relatives and acquaintances. 45So when they did not find Him, they returned to Jerusalem, seeking Him. 46Now so it was that after three days they found Him in the temple, sitting in the midst of the teachers, both listening to them and asking them questions. 47And all who heard Him were astonished at His understanding and answers. 48So when they saw Him, they were amazed; and His mother said to Him, "Son, why have You done this to us? Look, Your father and I have sought You anxiously."

49And He said to them, "Why did you seek Me? Did you not know that I must be about My Father's business?" 50But they did not understand the statement which He spoke to them.

2:33 a NU-Text reads And His father and mother.   2:37 a NU-Text reads a widow until she was eighty-four.
2:38 a NU-Text reads to God.   2:40 a NU-Text omits in spirit.   2:43 a NU-Text reads And His parents.

JESUS ADVANCES IN WISDOM AND FAVOR

⁵¹Then He went down with them and came to Nazareth, and was subject to them, but His mother kept all these things in her heart. ⁵²And Jesus increased in wisdom and stature, and in favor with God and men.

JOHN THE BAPTIST PREPARES THE WAY

3 Now in the fifteenth year of the reign of Tiberius Caesar, Pontius Pilate being governor of Judea, Herod being tetrarch of Galilee, his brother Philip tetrarch of Iturea and the region of Trachonitis, and Lysanias tetrarch of Abilene, ²while Annas and Caiaphas were high priests,ᵃ the word of God came to John the son of Zacharias in the wilderness. ³And he went into all the region around the Jordan, preaching a baptism of repentance for the remission of sins, ⁴as it is written in the book of the words of Isaiah the prophet, saying:

"The voice of one crying in the wilderness:
'Prepare the way of the LORD;
Make His paths straight.
5   Every valley shall be filled
And every mountain and hill brought low;

The crooked places shall be made straight
And the rough ways smooth;

6 And all flesh shall see the salvation of God."[a]

JOHN PREACHES TO THE PEOPLE

[7] Then he said to the multitudes that came out to be baptized by him, "Brood of vipers! Who warned you to flee from the wrath to come? [8] Therefore bear fruits worthy of repentance, and do not begin to say to yourselves, 'We have Abraham as *our* father.' For I say to you that God is able to raise up children to Abraham from these stones. [9] And even now the ax is laid to the root of the trees. Therefore every tree which does not bear good fruit is cut down and thrown into the fire."

[10] So the people asked him, saying, "What shall we do then?"

[11] He answered and said to them, "He who has two tunics, let him give to him who has none; and he who has food, let him do likewise."

[12] Then tax collectors also came to be baptized, and said to him, "Teacher, what shall we do?"

[13] And he said to them, "Collect no more than what is appointed for you."

[14] Likewise the soldiers asked him, saying, "And what shall we do?"

3:2 [a] NU-Text and M-Text read *in the high priesthood of Annas and Caiaphas.*   3:6 [a] Isaiah 40:3–5

LUKE 3:15

So he said to them, "Do not intimidate anyone or accuse falsely, and be content with your wages."

15Now as the people were in expectation, and all reasoned in their hearts about John, whether he was the Christ or not, 16John answered, saying to all, "I indeed baptize you with water; but One mightier than I is coming, whose sandal strap I am not worthy to loose. He will baptize you with the Holy Spirit and fire. 17His winnowing fan is in His hand, and He will thoroughly clean out His threshing floor, and gather the wheat into His barn; but the chaff He will burn with unquenchable fire."

18And with many other exhortations he preached to the people. 19But Herod the tetrarch, being rebuked by him concerning Herodias, his brother Philip's wife,[a] and for all the evils which Herod had done, 20also added this, above all, that he shut John up in prison.

JOHN BAPTIZES JESUS

21When all the people were baptized, it came to pass that Jesus also was baptized; and while He prayed, the heaven was opened. 22And the Holy Spirit descended in bodily form like a dove upon Him, and a voice came from heaven which said, "You are My beloved Son; in You I am well pleased."

THE GENEALOGY OF JESUS CHRIST

23Now Jesus Himself began *His ministry at* about thirty years of age, being (as was supposed) *the* son of Joseph, *the son* of Heli, 24*the son* of Matthat,[a] *the son* of Levi, *the son* of Melchi, *the son* of Janna, *the son* of Joseph, 25*the son* of Mattathiah, *the son* of Amos, *the son* of Nahum, *the son* of Esli, *the son* of Naggai, 26*the son* of Maath, *the son* of Mattathiah, *the son* of Semei, *the son* of Joseph, *the son* of Judah, 27*the son* of Joannas, *the son* of Rhesa, *the son* of Zerubbabel, *the son* of Shealtiel, *the son* of Neri, 28*the son* of Melchi, *the son* of Addi, *the son* of Cosam, *the son* of Elmodam, *the son* of Er, 29*the son* of Jose, *the son* of Eliezer, *the son* of Jorim, *the son* of Matthat, *the son* of Levi, 30*the son* of Simeon, *the son* of Judah, *the son* of Joseph, *the son* of Jonan, *the son* of Eliakim, 31*the son* of Melea, *the son* of Menan, *the son* of Mattathah, *the son* of Nathan, *the son* of David, 32*the son* of Jesse, *the son* of Obed, *the son* of Boaz, *the son* of Salmon, *the son* of Nahshon, 33*the son* of Amminadab, *the son* of Ram, *the son* of Hezron, *the son* of Perez, *the son* of Judah, 34*the son* of Jacob, *the son* of Isaac, *the son* of Abraham, *the son* of Terah, *the son* of Nahor, 35*the son* of Serug, *the son* of Reu, *the son* of Peleg, *the son* of Eber, *the son* of Shelah, 36*the son* of Cainan, *the son*

3:19 *a* NU-Text reads *his brother's wife.*   3:24 *a* This and several other names in the genealogy are spelled somewhat differently in the NU-Text. Since the New King James Version uses the Old Testament spelling for persons mentioned in the New Testament, these variations, which come from the Greek, have not been footnoted.

of Arphaxad, *the son of* Shem, *the son of* Noah, *the son of* Lamech, [37]*the son of* Methuselah, *the son of* Enoch, *the son of* Jared, *the son of* Mahalalel, *the son of* Cainan, [38]*the son of* Enosh, *the son of* Seth, *the son of* Adam, *the son of* God.

SATAN TEMPTS JESUS

4 Then Jesus, being filled with the Holy Spirit, returned from the Jordan and was led by the Spirit into[a] the wilderness, [2]being tempted for forty days by the devil. And in those days He ate nothing, and afterward, when they had ended, He was hungry.

[3]And the devil said to Him, "If You are the Son of God, command this stone to become bread."

[4]But Jesus answered him, saying,[a] "It is written, 'Man shall not live by bread alone, but by every word of God.'"[b]

[5]Then the devil, taking Him up on a high mountain, showed Him[a] all the kingdoms of the world in a moment of time. [6]And the devil said to Him, "All this authority I will give You, and their glory; for *this* has been delivered to me, and I give it to whomever I wish. [7]Therefore, if You will worship before me, all will be Yours."

[8]And Jesus answered and said to him, "Get behind Me, Satan![a] For[b] it is

written, 'You shall worship the LORD your God, and Him only you shall serve.'"[c]

9 Then he brought Him to Jerusalem, set Him on the pinnacle of the temple, and said to Him, "If You are the Son of God, throw Yourself down from here. 10 For it is written:

'He shall give His angels charge over you,
To keep you,'

11 and,

'In *their* hands they shall bear you up,
Lest you dash your foot against a stone.'"[a]

12 And Jesus answered and said to him, "It has been said, 'You shall not tempt the LORD your God.'"[a]

13 Now when the devil had ended every temptation, he departed from Him until an opportune time.

4:1 [a] NU-Text reads *In.*   4:4 [a] Deuteronomy 8:3   [b] NU-Text omits *but by every word of God.*
4:5 [a] NU-Text reads *And taking Him up, he showed Him.*   4:8 [a] NU-Text omits *Get behind Me, Satan.*
[b] NU-Text and M-Text omit *For.*   [c] Deuteronomy 6:13   4:11 [a] Psalm 91:11, 12   4:12 [a] Deuteronomy 6:16

LUKE 4:14

JESUS BEGINS HIS GALILEAN MINISTRY

¹⁴Then Jesus returned in the power of the Spirit to Galilee, and news of Him went out through all the surrounding region. ¹⁵And He taught in their synagogues, being glorified by all.

JESUS REJECTED AT NAZARETH

¹⁶So He came to Nazareth, where He had been brought up. And as His custom was, He went into the synagogue on the Sabbath day, and stood up to read. ¹⁷And He was handed the book of the prophet Isaiah. And when He had opened the book, He found the place where it was written:

18 "The Spirit of the LORD *is* upon Me,
  Because He has anointed Me
  To preach the gospel to *the* poor;
  He has sent Me to heal the brokenhearted,[a]
  To proclaim liberty to *the* captives
  And recovery of sight to *the* blind,
  To set at liberty those who are oppressed;
19 To proclaim the acceptable year of the LORD."[a]

20Then He closed the book, and gave *it* back to the attendant and sat down. And the eyes of all who were in the synagogue were fixed on Him. 21And He began to say to them, "Today this Scripture is fulfilled in your hearing." 22So all bore witness to Him, and marveled at the gracious words which proceeded out of His mouth. And they said, "Is this not Joseph's son?"

23He said to them, "You will surely say this proverb to Me, 'Physician, heal yourself! Whatever we have heard done in Capernaum,[a] do also here in Your country.'" 24Then He said, "Assuredly, I say to you, no prophet is accepted in his own country. 25But I tell you truly, many widows were in Israel in the days of Elijah, when the heaven was shut up three years and six months, and there was a great famine throughout all the land; 26but to none of them was Elijah sent except to Zarephath,[a] *in the region of* Sidon, to a woman *who was* a widow. 27And many lepers were in Israel in the time of Elisha the prophet, and none of them was cleansed except Naaman the Syrian."

28So all those in the synagogue, when they heard these things, were filled with wrath, 29and rose up and thrust Him out of the city; and they led Him to the brow of the hill on which their city was built, that they might throw Him down over the cliff. 30Then passing through the midst of them, He went His way.

4:18 [a] NU-Text omits *to heal the brokenhearted.*   4:19 [a] Isaiah 61:1, 2   4:23 [a] Here and elsewhere the NU-Text spelling is *Capharnaum.*   4:26 [a] Greek *Sarepta*

LUKE 4:31

JESUS CASTS OUT AN UNCLEAN SPIRIT

31Then He went down to Capernaum, a city of Galilee, and was teaching them on the Sabbaths. 32And they were astonished at His teaching, for His word was with authority. 33Now in the synagogue there was a man who had a spirit of an unclean demon. And he cried out with a loud voice, 34saying, "Let *us* alone! What have we to do with You, Jesus of Nazareth? Did You come to destroy us? I know who You are—the Holy One of God!"

35But Jesus rebuked him, saying, "Be quiet, and come out of him!" And when the demon had thrown him in *their* midst, it came out of him and did not hurt him. 36Then they were all amazed and spoke among themselves, saying, "What a word this *is!* For with authority and power He commands the unclean spirits, and they come out." 37And the report about Him went out into every place in the surrounding region.

PETER'S MOTHER-IN-LAW HEALED

38Now He arose from the synagogue and entered Simon's house. But Simon's wife's mother was sick with a high fever, and they made request of Him concerning her. 39So He stood over her and rebuked the fever, and it left her. And immediately she arose and served them.

MANY HEALED AFTER SABBATH SUNSET

40When the sun was setting, all those who had any that were sick with various diseases brought them to Him; and He laid His hands on every one of them and healed them. 41And demons also came out of many, crying out and saying, "You are the Christ,[a] the Son of God!"

And He, rebuking *them*, did not allow them to speak, for they knew that He was the Christ.

JESUS PREACHES IN GALILEE

42Now when it was day, He departed and went into a deserted place. And the crowd sought Him and came to Him, and tried to keep Him from leaving them; 43but He said to them, "I must preach the kingdom of God to the other cities also, because for this purpose I have been sent." 44And He was preaching in the synagogues of Galilee.[a]

FOUR FISHERMEN CALLED AS DISCIPLES

5 So it was, as the multitude pressed about Him to hear the word of God, that He stood by the Lake of Gennesaret, 2and saw two boats standing by the lake; but the fishermen had gone from them and were washing *their* nets. 3Then

4:41 [a] NU-Text omits *the Christ.*   4:44 [a] NU-Text reads *Judea.*

He got into one of the boats, which was Simon's, and asked him to put out a little from the land. And He sat down and taught the multitudes from the boat.

4When He had stopped speaking, He said to Simon, "Launch out into the deep and let down your nets for a catch."

5But Simon answered and said to Him, "Master, we have toiled all night and caught nothing; nevertheless at Your word I will let down the net." 6And when they had done this, they caught a great number of fish, and their net was breaking. 7So they signaled to *their* partners in the other boat to come and help them. And they came and filled both the boats, so that they began to sink. 8When Simon Peter saw *it,* he fell down at Jesus' knees, saying, "Depart from me, for I am a sinful man, O Lord!"

9For he and all who were with him were astonished at the catch of fish which they had taken; 10and so also *were* James and John, the sons of Zebedee, who were partners with Simon. And Jesus said to Simon, "Do not be afraid. From now on you will catch men." 11So when they had brought their boats to land, they forsook all and followed Him.

JESUS CLEANSES A LEPER

12And it happened when He was in a certain city, that behold, a man who was full of leprosy saw Jesus; and he fell on *his* face and implored Him, saying, "Lord, if You are willing, You can make me clean."

13Then He put out *His* hand and touched him, saying, "I am willing; be cleansed." Immediately the leprosy left him. 14And He charged him to tell no one, "But go and show yourself to the priest, and make an offering for your cleansing, as a testimony to them, just as Moses commanded."

15However, the report went around concerning Him all the more; and great multitudes came together to hear, and to be healed by Him of their infirmities. 16So He Himself *often* withdrew into the wilderness and prayed.

JESUS FORGIVES AND HEALS A PARALYTIC

17Now it happened on a certain day, as He was teaching, that there were Pharisees and teachers of the law sitting by, who had come out of every town of Galilee, Judea, and Jerusalem. And the power of the Lord was *present* to heal them.[a] 18Then behold, men brought on a bed a man who was paralyzed, whom they sought to bring in and lay before Him. 19And when they could not find how they might bring him in, because of the crowd, they went up on the housetop and let him down with *his* bed through the tiling into the midst before Jesus. 20When He saw their faith, He said to him, "Man, your sins are forgiven you."

5:17 *a* NU-Text reads *present with Him to heal.*

21And the scribes and the Pharisees began to reason, saying, "Who is this who speaks blasphemies? Who can forgive sins but God alone?"

22But when Jesus perceived their thoughts, He answered and said to them, "Why are you reasoning in your hearts? 23Which is easier, to say, 'Your sins are forgiven you,' or to say, 'Rise up and walk'? 24But that you may know that the Son of Man has power on earth to forgive sins"—He said to the man who was paralyzed, "I say to you, arise, take up your bed, and go to your house."

25Immediately he rose up before them, took up what he had been lying on, and departed to his own house, glorifying God. 26And they were all amazed, and they glorified God and were filled with fear, saying, "We have seen strange things today!"

MATTHEW THE TAX COLLECTOR

27After these things He went out and saw a tax collector named Levi, sitting at the tax office. And He said to him, "Follow Me." 28So he left all, rose up, and followed Him.

29Then Levi gave Him a great feast in his own house. And there were a great number of tax collectors and others who sat down with them. 30And their scribes and the Pharisees[a] complained against His disciples, saying, "Why do You eat and drink with tax collectors and sinners?"

31Jesus answered and said to them, "Those who are well have no need of a physician, but those who are sick. **32**I have not come to call *the* righteous, but sinners, to repentance."

JESUS IS QUESTIONED ABOUT FASTING

33Then they said to Him, "Why do[a] the disciples of John fast often and make prayers, and likewise those of the Pharisees, but Yours eat and drink?"

34And He said to them, "Can you make the friends of the bridegroom fast while the bridegroom is with them? **35**But the days will come when the bridegroom will be taken away from them; then they will fast in those days."

36Then He spoke a parable to them: "No one puts a piece from a new garment on an old one;[a] otherwise the new makes a tear, and also the piece that was *taken* out of the new does not match the old. **37**And no one puts new wine into old wineskins; or else the new wine will burst the wineskins and be spilled, and the wineskins will be ruined. **38**But new wine must be put into new wineskins, and both are preserved.[a] **39**And no one, having drunk old *wine,* immediately[a] desires new; for he says, 'The old is better.'"[b]

5:30 [a] NU-Text reads *But the Pharisees and their scribes.*   5:33 [a] NU-Text omits *Why do,* making the verse a statement.   5:36 [a] NU-Text reads *No one tears a piece from a new garment and puts it on an old one.*   5:38 [a] NU-Text omits *immediately.*   5:39 [a] NU-Text omits *and both are preserved.*   5:39 [a] NU-Text reads *good.*   [b] NU-Text reads *immediately.*

LUKE 6:1

JESUS IS LORD OF THE SABBATH

6 Now it happened on the second Sabbath after the first[a] that He went through the grainfields. And His disciples plucked the heads of grain and ate *them*, rubbing *them* in *their* hands. 2And some of the Pharisees said to them, "Why are you doing what is not lawful to do on the Sabbath?"

3But Jesus answering them said, "Have you not even read this, what David did when he was hungry, he and those who were with him: 4how he went into the house of God, took and ate the showbread, and also gave some to those with him, which is not lawful for any but the priests to eat?" 5And He said to them, "The Son of Man is also Lord of the Sabbath."

HEALING ON THE SABBATH

6Now it happened on another Sabbath, also, that He entered the synagogue and taught. And a man was there whose right hand was withered. 7So the scribes and Pharisees watched Him closely, whether He would heal on the Sabbath, that they might find an accusation against Him. 8But He knew their thoughts, and said to the man who had the withered hand, "Arise and stand here." And he arose and stood. 9Then Jesus said to them, "I will ask you one thing: Is it lawful on the Sabbath to do good or to do evil, to save life or to destroy?"a 10And when

He had looked around at them all, He said to the man,[a] "Stretch out your hand." And he did so, and his hand was restored as whole as the other.[b] 11But they were filled with rage, and discussed with one another what they might do to Jesus.

THE TWELVE APOSTLES

12Now it came to pass in those days that He went out to the mountain to pray, and continued all night in prayer to God. 13And when it was day, He called His disciples to *Himself;* and from them He chose twelve whom He also named apostles: 14Simon, whom He also named Peter, and Andrew his brother; James and John; Philip and Bartholomew; 15Matthew and Thomas; James the *son of* Alphaeus, and Simon called the Zealot; 16Judas *the son of* James, and Judas Iscariot who also became a traitor.

JESUS HEALS A GREAT MULTITUDE

17And He came down with them and stood on a level place with a crowd of His disciples and a great multitude of people from all Judea and Jerusalem, and from the seacoast of Tyre and Sidon, who came to hear Him and be healed of their diseases, 18as well as those who were tormented with unclean spirits. And

6:1 a NU-Text reads *on a Sabbath.*   6:9 a M-Text reads *to kill.*   6:10 a NU-Text and M-Text read *to him.*
6:10 a NU-Text omits *as whole as the other.*

they were healed. 19And the whole multitude sought to touch Him, for power went out from Him and healed *them* all.

THE BEATITUDES

20Then He lifted up His eyes toward His disciples, and said:

"Blessed *are you* poor,
For yours is the kingdom of God.
21 Blessed *are you* who hunger now,
For you shall be filled.
Blessed *are you* who weep now,
For you shall laugh.
22 Blessed are you when men hate you,
And when they exclude you,
And revile *you*, and cast out your name as evil,
For the Son of Man's sake.
23 Rejoice in that day and leap for joy!
For indeed your reward *is* great in heaven,
For in like manner their fathers did to the prophets.

JESUS PRONOUNCES WOES

24 "But woe to you who are rich,
    For you have received your consolation.
25 Woe to you who are full,
    For you shall hunger.
    Woe to you who laugh now,
    For you shall mourn and weep.
26 Woe to you[a] when all[b] men speak well of you,
    For so did their fathers to the false prophets.

LOVE YOUR ENEMIES

27 "But I say to you who hear: Love your enemies, do good to those who hate you, 28bless those who curse you, and pray for those who spitefully use you. 29To him who strikes you on the *one* cheek, offer the other also. And from him who takes away your cloak, do not withhold *your* tunic either. 30Give to everyone who asks of you. And from him who takes away your goods do not ask *them* back. 31And just as you want men to do to you, you also do to them likewise.

32 "But if you love those who love you, what credit is that to you? For even sinners love those who love them. 33 And if you do good to those who do good

6:26 [a] NU-Text and M-Text omit *to you.* [b] M-Text omits *all.*

LUKE 6:34

to you, what credit is that to you? For even sinners do the same. ³⁴And if you lend *to those* from whom you hope to receive back, what credit is that to you? For even sinners lend to sinners to receive as much back. ³⁵But love your enemies, do good, and lend, hoping for nothing in return; and your reward will be great, and you will be sons of the Most High. For He is kind to the unthankful and evil. ³⁶Therefore be merciful, just as your Father also is merciful.

DO NOT JUDGE

³⁷"Judge not, and you shall not be judged. Condemn not, and you shall not be condemned. Forgive, and you will be forgiven. ³⁸Give, and it will be given to you: good measure, pressed down, shaken together, and running over will be put into your bosom. For with the same measure that you use, it will be measured back to you."

³⁹And He spoke a parable to them: "Can the blind lead the blind? Will they not both fall into the ditch? ⁴⁰A disciple is not above his teacher, but everyone who is perfectly trained will be like his teacher. ⁴¹And why do you look at the speck in your brother's eye, but do not perceive the plank in your own eye? ⁴²Or how can you say to your brother, 'Brother, let me remove the speck that *is* in your eye,' when you yourself do not see the plank that *is* in your own eye?

Hypocrite! First remove the plank from your own eye, and then you will see clearly to remove the speck that is in your brother's eye.

A TREE IS KNOWN BY ITS FRUIT

43"For a good tree does not bear bad fruit, nor does a bad tree bear good fruit. 44For every tree is known by its own fruit. For *men* do not gather figs from thorns, nor do they gather grapes from a bramble bush. 45A good man out of the good treasure of his heart brings forth good; and an evil man out of the evil treasure of his heart[a] brings forth evil. For out of the abundance of the heart his mouth speaks.

BUILD ON THE ROCK

46"But why do you call Me 'Lord, Lord,' and not do the things which I say? 47Whoever comes to Me, and hears My sayings and does them, I will show you whom he is like: 48He is like a man building a house, who dug deep and laid the foundation on the rock. And when the flood arose, the stream beat vehemently against that house, and could not shake it, for it was founded on the rock.[a] 49But he who heard and did nothing is like a man who built a house on

6:45 [a] NU-Text omits *treasure of his heart.*   6:48 [a] NU-Text reads *for it was well built.*

the earth without a foundation, against which the stream beat vehemently; and immediately it fell. ª And the ruin of that house was great."

JESUS HEALS A CENTURION'S SERVANT

7 Now when He concluded all His sayings in the hearing of the people, He entered Capernaum. ²And a certain centurion's servant, who was dear to him, was sick and ready to die. ³So when he heard about Jesus, he sent elders of the Jews to Him, pleading with Him to come and heal his servant. ⁴And when they came to Jesus, they begged Him earnestly, saying that the one for whom He should do this was deserving, ⁵"for he loves our nation, and has built us a synagogue."

⁶Then Jesus went with them. And when He was already not far from the house, the centurion sent friends to Him, saying to Him, "Lord, do not trouble Yourself, for I am not worthy that You should enter under my roof. ⁷Therefore I did not even think myself worthy to come to You. But say the word, and my servant will be healed. ⁸For I also am a man placed under authority, having soldiers under me. And I say to one, 'Go,' and he goes; and to another, 'Come,' and he comes; and to my servant, 'Do this,' and he does *it*."

⁹When Jesus heard these things, He marveled at him, and turned around

and said to the crowd that followed Him, "I say to you, I have not found such great faith, not even in Israel!" [10]And those who were sent, returning to the house, found the servant well who had been sick.[a]

JESUS RAISES THE SON OF THE WIDOW OF NAIN

[11]Now it happened, the day after, *that* He went into a city called Nain; and many of His disciples went with Him, and a large crowd. [12]And when He came near the gate of the city, behold, a dead man was being carried out, the only son of his mother; and she was a widow. And a large crowd from the city was with her. [13]When the Lord saw her, He had compassion on her and said to her, "Do not weep." [14]Then He came and touched the open coffin, and those who carried *him* stood still. And He said, "Young man, I say to you, arise." [15]So he who was dead sat up and began to speak. And He presented him to his mother.

[16]Then fear came upon all, and they glorified God, saying, "A great prophet has risen up among us"; and, "God has visited His people." [17]And this report about Him went throughout all Judea and all the surrounding region.

JOHN THE BAPTIST SENDS MESSENGERS TO JESUS

[18]Then the disciples of John reported to him concerning all these things.

6:49 [a] NU-Text reads *collapsed.*   7:10 [a] NU-Text omits *who had been sick.*

19And John, calling two of his disciples to *him*, sent *them* to Jesus,*a* saying, "Are You the Coming One, or do we look for another?"

20When the men had come to Him, they said, "John the Baptist has sent us to You, saying, 'Are You the Coming One, or do we look for another?'" 21And that very hour He cured many of infirmities, afflictions, and evil spirits; and to many blind He gave sight.

22Jesus answered and said to them, "Go and tell John the things you have seen and heard: that *the* blind see, *the* lame walk, *the* lepers are cleansed, *the* deaf hear, *the* dead are raised, *the* poor have the gospel preached to them. 23And blessed is *he* who is not offended because of Me."

24When the messengers of John had departed, He began to speak to the multitudes concerning John: "What did you go out into the wilderness to see? A reed shaken by the wind? 25But what did you go out to see? A man clothed in soft garments? Indeed those who are gorgeously appareled and live in luxury are in kings' courts. 26But what did you go out to see? A prophet? Yes, I say to you, and more than a prophet. 27This is *he* of whom it is written:

'Behold, I send My messenger before Your face,
    Who will prepare Your way before You.'*a*

28For I say to you, among those born of women there is not a greater prophet than John the Baptist;[a] but he who is least in the kingdom of God is greater than he." 29And when all the people heard *Him*, even the tax collectors justified God, having been baptized with the baptism of John. 30But the Pharisees and lawyers rejected the will of God for themselves, not having been baptized by him.

31And the Lord said,[a] "To what then shall I liken the men of this generation, and what are they like? 32They are like children sitting in the marketplace and calling to one another, saying:

'We played the flute for you,
    And you did not dance;
We mourned to you,
    And you did not weep.'

33For John the Baptist came neither eating bread nor drinking wine, and you say, 'He has a demon.' 34The Son of Man has come eating and drinking, and you say, 'Look, a glutton and a winebibber, a friend of tax collectors and sinners!' 35But wisdom is justified by all her children."

7:19 [a] NU-Text reads *the Lord.*   7:27 [a] Malachi 3:1   7:28 [a] NU-Text reads *there is none greater than John.*
7:31 [a] NU-Text and M-Text omit *And the Lord said.*

A SINFUL WOMAN FORGIVEN

36Then one of the Pharisees asked Him to eat with him. And He went to the Pharisee's house, and sat down to eat. 37And behold, a woman in the city who was a sinner, when she knew that *Jesus* sat at the table in the Pharisee's house, brought an alabaster flask of fragrant oil, 38and stood at His feet behind *Him* weeping; and she began to wash His feet with her tears, and wiped *them* with the hair of her head; and she kissed His feet and anointed *them* with the fragrant oil. 39Now when the Pharisee who had invited Him saw *this*, he spoke to himself, saying, "This Man, if He were a prophet, would know who and what manner of woman *this is* who is touching Him, for she is a sinner."

40And Jesus answered and said to him, "Simon, I have something to say to you."

So he said, "Teacher, say it."

41"There was a certain creditor who had two debtors. One owed five hundred denarii, and the other fifty. 42And when they had nothing with which to repay, he freely forgave them both. Tell Me, therefore, which of them will love him more?"

43Simon answered and said, "I suppose the *one* whom he forgave more."

And He said to him, "You have rightly judged." 44Then He turned to the woman and said to Simon, "Do you see this woman? I entered your house; you gave

Me no water for My feet, but she has washed My feet with her tears and wiped *them* with the hair of her head. 45You gave Me no kiss, but this woman has not ceased to kiss My feet since the time I came in. 46You did not anoint My head with oil, but this woman has anointed My feet with fragrant oil. 47Therefore I say to you, her sins, which *are* many, are forgiven, for she loved much. But to whom little is forgiven, *the same* loves little."

48Then He said to her, "Your sins are forgiven."

49And those who sat at the table with Him began to say to themselves, "Who is this who even forgives sins?"

50Then He said to the woman, "Your faith has saved you. Go in peace."

MANY WOMEN MINISTER TO JESUS

8 Now it came to pass, afterward, that He went through every city and village, preaching and bringing the glad tidings of the kingdom of God. And the twelve *were* with Him, 2and certain women who had been healed of evil spirits and infirmities—Mary called Magdalene, out of whom had come seven demons, 3and Joanna the wife of Chuza, Herod's steward, and Susanna, and many others who provided for Him[a] from their substance.

8:3 [a] NU-Text and M-Text read *them*.

THE PARABLE OF THE SOWER

4And when a great multitude had gathered, and they had come to Him from every city, He spoke by a parable: 5"A sower went out to sow his seed. And as he sowed, some fell by the wayside; and it was trampled down, and the birds of the air devoured it. 6Some fell on rock; and as soon as it sprang up, it withered away because it lacked moisture. 7And some fell among thorns, and the thorns sprang up with it and choked it. 8But others fell on good ground, sprang up, and yielded a crop a hundredfold." When He had said these things He cried, "He who has ears to hear, let him hear!"

THE PURPOSE OF PARABLES

9Then His disciples asked Him, saying, "What does this parable mean?" 10And He said, "To you it has been given to know the mysteries of the king- dom of God, but to the rest *it is given* in parables, that

'Seeing they may not see,
    And hearing they may not understand.'*a*

THE PARABLE OF THE SOWER EXPLAINED

11"Now the parable is this: The seed is the word of God. 12Those by the wayside are the ones who hear; then the devil comes and takes away the word out of their hearts, lest they should believe and be saved. 13But the ones on the rock *are those* who, when they hear, receive the word with joy; and these have no root, who believe for a while and in time of temptation fall away. 14Now the ones *that* fell among thorns are those who, when they have heard, go out and are choked with cares, riches, and pleasures of life, and bring no fruit to maturity. 15But the ones *that* fell on the good ground are those who, having heard the word with a noble and good heart, keep *it* and bear fruit with patience.

THE PARABLE OF THE REVEALED LIGHT

16"No one, when he has lit a lamp, covers it with a vessel or puts *it* under a bed, but sets *it* on a lampstand, that those who enter may see the light. 17For nothing is secret that will not be revealed, nor *anything* hidden that will not be known and come to light. 18Therefore take heed how you hear. For whoever has, to him *more* will be given; and whoever does not have, even what he seems to have will be taken from him."

8:10 *a* Isaiah 6:9

LUKE 8:19

JESUS' MOTHER AND BROTHERS COME TO HIM

19Then His mother and brothers came to Him, and could not approach Him because of the crowd. 20And it was told Him *by some*, who said, "Your mother and Your brothers are standing outside, desiring to see You."

21But He answered and said to them, "My mother and My brothers are these who hear the word of God and do it."

WIND AND WAVE OBEY JESUS

22Now it happened, on a certain day, that He got into a boat with His disciples. And He said to them, "Let us cross over to the other side of the lake." And they launched out. 23But as they sailed He fell asleep. And a windstorm came down on the lake, and they were filling *with water*, and were in jeopardy. 24And they came to Him and awoke Him, saying, "Master, Master, we are perishing!"

Then He arose and rebuked the wind and the raging of the water. And they ceased, and there was a calm. 25But He said to them, "Where is your faith?"

And they were afraid, and marveled, saying to one another, "Who can this be? For He commands even the winds and water, and they obey Him!"

A DEMON-POSSESSED MAN HEALED

[26]Then they sailed to the country of the Gadarenes,[a] which is opposite Galilee. [27]And when He stepped out on the land, there met Him a certain man from the city who had demons for a long time. And he wore no clothes,[a] nor did he live in a house but in the tombs. [28]When he saw Jesus, he cried out, fell down before Him, and with a loud voice said, "What have I to do with You, Jesus, Son of the Most High God? I beg You, do not torment me!" [29]For He had commanded the unclean spirit to come out of the man. For it had often seized him, and he was kept under guard, bound with chains and shackles; and he broke the bonds and was driven by the demon into the wilderness.

[30]Jesus asked him, saying, "What is your name?"

And he said, "Legion," because many demons had entered him. [31]And they begged Him that He would not command them to go out into the abyss.

[32]Now a herd of many swine was feeding there on the mountain. So they begged Him that He would permit them to enter them. And He permitted them. [33]Then the demons went out of the man and entered the swine, and the herd ran violently down the steep place into the lake and drowned.

[34]When those who fed *them* saw what had happened, they fled and told *it*

8:26 [a] NU-Text reads *Gerasenes.*   8:27 [a] NU-Text reads *who had demons and for a long time wore no clothes.*

in the city and in the country. 35Then they went out to see what had happened, and came to Jesus, and found the man from whom the demons had departed, sitting at the feet of Jesus, clothed and in his right mind. And they were afraid. 36They also who had seen *it* told them by what means he who had been demon-possessed was healed. 37Then the whole multitude of the surrounding region of the Gadarenes[a] asked Him to depart from them, for they were seized with great fear. And He got into the boat and returned.

38Now the man from whom the demons had departed begged Him that he might be with Him. But Jesus sent him away, saying, 39"Return to your own house, and tell what great things God has done for you." And he went his way and proclaimed throughout the whole city what great things Jesus had done for him.

A GIRL RESTORED TO LIFE AND A WOMAN HEALED

40So it was, when Jesus returned, that the multitude welcomed Him, for they were all waiting for Him. 41And behold, there came a man named Jairus, and he was a ruler of the synagogue. And he fell down at Jesus' feet and begged Him to come to his house, 42for he had an only daughter about twelve years of age, and she was dying.

But as He went, the multitudes thronged Him. 43Now a woman, having a flow of blood for twelve years, who had spent all her livelihood on physicians and could not be healed by any, ⁴⁴came from behind and touched the border of His garment. And immediately her flow of blood stopped.

⁴⁵And Jesus said, "Who touched Me?"

When all denied it, Peter and those with him[a] said, "Master, the multitudes throng and press You, and You say, 'Who touched Me?'"[b]

⁴⁶But Jesus said, "Somebody touched Me, for I perceived power going out from Me." ⁴⁷Now when the woman saw that she was not hidden, she came trembling; and falling down before Him, she declared to Him in the presence of all the people the reason she had touched Him and how she was healed immediately. ⁴⁸And He said to her, "Daughter, be of good cheer;[a] your faith has made you well. Go in peace."

⁴⁹While He was still speaking, someone came from the ruler of the synagogue's *house*, saying to him, "Your daughter is dead. Do not trouble the Teacher."[a]

⁵⁰But when Jesus heard *it*, He answered him, saying, "Do not be afraid; only believe, and she will be made well." ⁵¹When He came into the house, He permitted no one to go in[a] except Peter, James, and John,[b] and the father and mother of

8:37 [a] NU-Text reads *Gerasenes*.   8:45 [a] NU-Text omits *and those with him*.   [b] NU-Text omits *You say, 'Who touched Me?'*   8:48 [a] NU-Text omits *be of good cheer*.   8:49 [a] NU-Text adds *anymore*.
8:51 [a] NU-Text adds *with Him*.   [b] NU-Text and M-Text read *Peter, John, and James*.

the girl. 52Now all wept and mourned for her; but He said, "Do not weep; she is not dead, but sleeping." 53And they ridiculed Him, knowing that she was dead. 54But He put them all outside,ᵃ took her by the hand and called, saying, "Little girl, arise." 55Then her spirit returned, and she arose immediately. And He commanded that she be given *something* to eat. 56And her parents were astonished, but He charged them to tell no one what had happened.

SENDING OUT THE TWELVE

9 Then He called His twelve disciples together and gave them power and authority over all demons, and to cure diseases. 2He sent them to preach the kingdom of God and to heal the sick. 3And He said to them, "Take nothing for the journey, neither staffs nor bag nor bread nor money; and do not have two tunics apiece.

4"Whatever house you enter, stay there, and from there depart. 5And whoever will not receive you, when you go out of that city, shake off the very dust from your feet as a testimony against them."

6So they departed and went through the towns, preaching the gospel and healing everywhere.

HEROD SEEKS TO SEE JESUS

7Now Herod the tetrarch heard of all that was done by Him; and he was perplexed, because it was said by some that John had risen from the dead, 8and by some that Elijah had appeared, and by others that one of the old prophets had risen again. 9Herod said, "John I have beheaded, but who is this of whom I hear such things?" So he sought to see Him.

FEEDING THE FIVE THOUSAND

10And the apostles, when they had returned, told Him all that they had done. Then He took them and went aside privately into a deserted place belonging to the city called Bethsaida. 11But when the multitudes knew *it*, they followed Him; and He received them and spoke to them about the kingdom of God, and healed those who had need of healing. 12When the day began to wear away, the twelve came and said to Him, "Send the multitude away, that they may go into the surrounding towns and country, and lodge and get provisions; for we are in a deserted place here."

13But He said to them, "You give them something to eat."

And they said, "We have no more than five loaves and two fish, unless we go and buy food for all these people." 14For there were about five thousand men.

8:54 a NU-Text omits *put them all outside.*

Then He said to His disciples, "Make them sit down in groups of fifty." ¹⁵And they did so, and made them all sit down.

¹⁶Then He took the five loaves and the two fish, and looking up to heaven, He blessed and broke them, and gave *them* to the disciples to set before the multitude. ¹⁷So they all ate and were filled, and twelve baskets of the leftover fragments were taken up by them.

PETER CONFESSES JESUS AS THE CHRIST

¹⁸And it happened, as He was alone praying, *that* His disciples joined Him, and He asked them, saying, "Who do the crowds say that I am?"

¹⁹So they answered and said, "John the Baptist, but some *say* Elijah; and others *say* that one of the old prophets has risen again."

²⁰He said to them, "But who do you say that I am?"

Peter answered and said, "The Christ of God."

JESUS PREDICTS HIS DEATH AND RESURRECTION

²¹And He strictly warned and commanded them to tell this to no one, ²²saying, "The Son of Man must suffer many things, and be rejected by the elders and chief priests and scribes, and be killed, and be raised the third day."

58And Jesus said to him, "Foxes have holes and birds of the air *have* nests, but the Son of Man has nowhere to lay *His* head."

59Then He said to another, "Follow Me."

But he said, "Lord, let me first go and bury my father."

60Jesus said to him, "Let the dead bury their own dead,[a] but you go and preach the kingdom of God."

61And another also said, "Lord, I will follow You, but let me first go *and* bid them farewell who are at my house."

62But Jesus said to him, "No one, having put his hand to the plow, and looking back, is fit for the kingdom of God."

THE SEVENTY SENT OUT

10 After these things the Lord appointed seventy others also,[a] and sent them two by two before His face into every city and place where He Himself was about to go. 2Then He said to them, "The harvest truly *is* great, but the laborers *are* few; therefore pray the Lord of the harvest to send out laborers into His harvest. 3Go your way; behold, I send you out as lambs among wolves.

9:50 a NU-Text reads *you*.   b NU-Text omits the rest of this verse.   9:54 a NU-Text omits *just as Elijah did.*
9:55 a NU-Text omits the rest of this verse.   9:56 a NU-Text omits the first sentence of this verse.
10:1 a NU-Text reads *seventy-two others.*

4Carry neither money bag, knapsack, nor sandals; and greet no one along the road. 5But whatever house you enter, first say, 'Peace to this house.' 6And if a son of peace is there, your peace will rest on it; if not, it will return to you. 7And remain in the same house, eating and drinking such things as they give, for the laborer is worthy of his wages. Do not go from house to house. 8Whatever city you enter, and they receive you, eat such things as are set before you. 9And heal the sick there, and say to them, 'The kingdom of God has come near to you.' 10But whatever city you enter, and they do not receive you, go out into its streets and say, 11'The very dust of your city which clings to us*a* we wipe off against you. Nevertheless know this, that the kingdom of God has come near you.' 12But*a* I say to you that it will be more tolerable in that Day for Sodom than for that city.

WOE TO THE IMPENITENT CITIES

13"Woe to you, Chorazin! Woe to you, Bethsaida! For if the mighty works which were done in you had been done in Tyre and Sidon, they would have repented long ago, sitting in sackcloth and ashes. 14But it will be more tolerable for Tyre and Sidon at the judgment than for you. 15And you, Capernaum, who are exalted to heaven, will be brought down to Hades.*a* 16He who hears you hears Me, he who rejects you rejects Me, and he who rejects Me rejects Him who sent Me."

THE SEVENTY RETURN WITH JOY

[17]Then the seventy[a] returned with joy, saying, "Lord, even the demons are subject to us in Your name."

[18]And He said to them, "I saw Satan fall like lightning from heaven. [19]Behold, I give you the authority to trample on serpents and scorpions, and over all the power of the enemy, and nothing shall by any means hurt you. [20]Nevertheless do not rejoice in this, that the spirits are subject to you, but rather[a] rejoice because your names are written in heaven."

JESUS REJOICES IN THE SPIRIT

[21]In that hour Jesus rejoiced in the Spirit and said, "I thank You, Father, Lord of heaven and earth, that You have hidden these things from the wise and prudent and revealed them to babes. Even so, Father, for so it seemed good in Your sight. [22]All[a] things have been delivered to Me by My Father, and no one knows who the Son is except the Father, and who the Father is except the Son, and the one to whom the Son wills to reveal Him."

[23]Then He turned to His disciples and said privately, "Blessed are the eyes

10:11 [a] NU-Text reads our feet.   10:12 [a] NU-Text and M-Text omit But.   10:15 [a] NU-Text reads will you be exalted to heaven? You will be thrust down to Hades!   10:17 [a] NU-Text reads seventy-two. 10:20 [a] NU-Text and M-Text omit rather.   10:22 [a] M-Text reads And turning to the disciples He said, "All . . . .

which see the things you see; 24for I tell you that many prophets and kings have desired to see what you see, and have not seen *it*, and to hear what you hear, and have not heard *it*."

THE PARABLE OF THE GOOD SAMARITAN

25And behold, a certain lawyer stood up and tested Him, saying, "Teacher, what shall I do to inherit eternal life?"

26He said to him, "What is written in the law? What is your reading *of it?*"

27So he answered and said, "'You shall love the LORD your God with all your heart, with all your soul, with all your strength, and with all your mind,'a and 'your neighbor as yourself.'b

28And He said to him, "You have answered rightly; do this and you will live."

29But he, wanting to justify himself, said to Jesus, "And who is my neighbor?"

30Then Jesus answered and said: "A certain *man* went down from Jerusalem to Jericho, and fell among thieves, who stripped him of his clothing, wounded *him*, and departed, leaving *him* half dead. 31Now by chance a certain priest came down that road. And when he saw him, he passed by on the other side. 32Likewise a Levite, when he arrived at the place, came and looked, and passed by on the other side. 33But a certain Samaritan, as he journeyed, came where he was. And when he saw him, he had compassion. 34So he went to *him* and bandaged his wounds, pouring on oil and wine; and he set him on his own animal, brought him to an inn, and took care of him. 35On the next day, when he departed,[a] he took out two denarii, gave *them* to the innkeeper, and said to him, 'Take care of him; and whatever more you spend, when I come again, I will repay you.' 36So which of these three do you think was neighbor to him who fell among the thieves?"

37And he said, "He who showed mercy on him."

Then Jesus said to him, "Go and do likewise."

MARY AND MARTHA WORSHIP AND SERVE

38Now it happened as they went that He entered a certain village; and a certain woman named Martha welcomed Him into her house. 39And she had a sister called Mary, who also sat at Jesus'[a] feet and heard His word. 40But Martha was distracted with much serving, and she approached Him and said, "Lord, do You not care that my sister has left me to serve alone? Therefore tell her to help me."

41And Jesus[a] answered and said to her, "Martha, Martha, you are worried and troubled about many things. 42But one thing is needed, and Mary has chosen that good part, which will not be taken away from her."

10:27 [a] Deuteronomy 6:5   [b] Leviticus 19:18   10:35 [a] NU-Text omits *when he departed.*   10:39 [a] NU-Text reads *the Lord.*   10:41 [a] NU-Text reads *the Lord's.*

THE MODEL PRAYER

11 Now it came to pass, as He was praying in a certain place, when He ceased, *that* one of His disciples said to Him, "Lord, teach us to pray, as John also taught his disciples."

2 So He said to them, "When you pray, say:

Our Father in heaven,[a]
Hallowed be Your name.
Your kingdom come.[b]
Your will be done
    On earth as *it is* in heaven.

3 Give us day by day our daily bread.
4 And forgive us our sins,
For we also forgive everyone who is indebted to us.
And do not lead us into temptation,
But deliver us from the evil one."[a]

A FRIEND COMES AT MIDNIGHT

5 And He said to them, "Which of you shall have a friend, and go to him at

midnight and say to him, 'Friend, lend me three loaves; ⁶for a friend of mine has come to me on his journey, and I have nothing to set before him'; ⁷and he will answer from within and say, 'Do not trouble me; the door is now shut, and my children are with me in bed; I cannot rise and give to you'? ⁸I say to you, though he will not rise and give to him because he is his friend, yet because of his persistence he will rise and give him as many as he needs.

KEEP ASKING, SEEKING, KNOCKING

⁹"So I say to you, ask, and it will be given to you; seek, and you will find; knock, and it will be opened to you. ¹⁰For everyone who asks receives, and he who seeks finds, and to him who knocks it will be opened. ¹¹If a son asks for bread*ᵃ* from any father among you, will he give him a stone? Or *if he asks* for a fish, will he give him a serpent instead of a fish? ¹²Or if he asks for an egg, will he offer him a scorpion? ¹³If you then, being evil, know how to give good gifts to your children, how much more will *your* heavenly Father give the Holy Spirit to those who ask Him!"

A HOUSE DIVIDED CANNOT STAND

¹⁴And He was casting out a demon, and it was mute. So it was, when the demon

11:2 *ᵃ* NU-Text omits *Our* and *in heaven.* *ᵇ* NU-Text omits the rest of this verse. 11:4 *ᵃ* NU-Text *But deliver us from the evil one.* 11:11 *ᵃ* NU-Text omits from *bread* through *for* in the next sentence.

had gone out, that the mute spoke; and the multitudes marveled. 15But some of them said, "He casts out demons by Beelzebub,ª the ruler of the demons."

16Others, testing *Him*, sought from Him a sign from heaven. 17But He, knowing their thoughts, said to them: "Every kingdom divided against itself is brought to desolation, and a house *divided* against a house falls. 18If Satan also is divided against himself, how will his kingdom stand? Because you say I cast out demons by Beelzebub. 19And if I cast out demons by Beelzebub, by whom do your sons cast *them* out? Therefore they will be your judges. 20But if I cast out demons with the finger of God, surely the kingdom of God has come upon you. 21When a strong man, fully armed, guards his own palace, his goods are in peace. 22But when a stronger than he comes upon him and overcomes him, he takes from him all his armor in which he trusted, and divides his spoils. 23He who is not with Me is against Me, and he who does not gather with Me scatters.

AN UNCLEAN SPIRIT RETURNS

24"When an unclean spirit goes out of a man, he goes through dry places, seeking rest; and finding none, he says, 'I will return to my house from which I came.' 25And when he comes, he finds *it* swept and put in order. 26Then he goes and takes with *him* seven other spirits more wicked than himself, and they enter and dwell there; and the last *state* of that man is worse than the first."

KEEPING THE WORD

27 And it happened, as He spoke these things, that a certain woman from the crowd raised her voice and said to Him, "Blessed *is* the womb that bore You, and *the* breasts which nursed You!"

28 But He said, "More than that, blessed *are* those who hear the word of God and keep it!"

SEEKING A SIGN

29 And while the crowds were thickly gathered together, He began to say, "This is an evil generation. It seeks a sign, and no sign will be given to it except the sign of Jonah the prophet.^a 30 For as Jonah became a sign to the Ninevites, so also the Son of Man will be to this generation. 31 The queen of the South will rise up in the judgment with the men of this generation and condemn them, for she came from the ends of the earth to hear the wisdom of Solomon; and indeed a greater than Solomon *is* here. 32 The men of Nineveh will rise up in the judgment with this generation and condemn it, for they repented at the preaching of Jonah; and indeed a greater than Jonah *is* here.

11:15 ^a NU-Text and M-Text read *Beelzebul.*   11:29 ^a NU-Text omits *the prophet.*

LUKE 11:33

THE LAMP OF THE BODY

33"No one, when he has lit a lamp, puts *it* in a secret place or under a basket, but on a lampstand, that those who come in may see the light. 34The lamp of the body is the eye. Therefore, when *your eye* is good, your whole body also is full of light. But when *your eye* is bad, your body also is full of darkness. 35Therefore take heed that the light which is in you is not darkness. 36If then your whole body *is* full of light, having no part dark, *the whole body* will be full of light, as when the bright shining of a lamp gives you light."

WOE TO THE PHARISEES AND LAWYERS

37And as He spoke, a certain Pharisee asked Him to dine with him. So He went in and sat down to eat. 38When the Pharisee saw *it*, he marveled that He had not first washed before dinner.

39Then the Lord said to him, "Now you Pharisees make the outside of the cup and dish clean, but your inward part is full of greed and wickedness. 40Foolish ones! Did not He who made the outside make the inside also? 41But rather give alms of such things as you have; then indeed all things are clean to you.

42"But woe to you Pharisees! For you tithe the mint and rue and all manner of herbs, and pass by justice and the love of God. These you ought to have done, without leaving the others undone. 43Woe to you Pharisees! For you love the best seats in the synagogues and greetings in the marketplaces. 44Woe to you, scribes and Pharisees, hypocrites![a] For you are like graves which are not seen, and the men who walk over *them are not aware of them.*

45Then one of the lawyers answered and said to Him, "Teacher, by saying these things You reproach us also."

46And He said, "Woe to you also, lawyers! For you load men with burdens hard to bear, and you yourselves do not touch the burdens with one of your fingers. 47Woe to you! For you build the tombs of the prophets, and your fathers killed them. 48In fact, you bear witness that you approve the deeds of your fathers; for they indeed killed them, and you build their tombs. 49Therefore the wisdom of God also said, 'I will send prophets and apostles, and *some* of them they will kill and persecute,' 50that the blood of all the prophets which was shed from the foundation of the world may be required of this generation, 51from the blood of Abel to the blood of Zechariah who perished between the altar and the temple. Yes, I say to you, it shall be required of this generation.

52"Woe to you lawyers! For you have taken away the key of knowledge. You did not enter in yourselves, and those who were entering in you hindered."

53And as He said these things to them,[a] the scribes and the Pharisees began

11:44 [a] NU-Text omits *scribes and Pharisees, hypocrites.*   11:53 [a] NU-Text reads *And when He left there.*

to assail *Him* vehemently, and to cross-examine Him about many things, ⁵⁴lying in wait for Him, and seeking to catch Him in something He might say, that they might accuse Him.ᵃ

BEWARE OF HYPOCRISY

12 In the meantime, when an innumerable multitude of people had gathered together, so that they trampled one another, He began to say to His disciples first *of all,* "Beware of the leaven of the Pharisees, which is hypocrisy. ²For there is nothing covered that will not be revealed, nor hidden that will not be known. ³Therefore whatever you have spoken in the dark will be heard in the light, and what you have spoken in the ear in inner rooms will be proclaimed on the housetops.

JESUS TEACHES THE FEAR OF GOD

⁴"And I say to you, My friends, do not be afraid of those who kill the body, and after that have no more that they can do. ⁵But I will show you whom you should fear: Fear Him who, after He has killed, has power to cast into hell; yes, I say to you, fear Him!

⁶"Are not five sparrows sold for two copper coins?ᵃ And not one of them is forgotten before God. ⁷But the very hairs of your head are all numbered. Do

not fear therefore; you are of more value than many sparrows.

CONFESS CHRIST BEFORE MEN

8"Also I say to you, whoever confesses Me before men, him the Son of Man also will confess before the angels of God. 9But he who denies Me before men will be denied before the angels of God.

10"And anyone who speaks a word against the Son of Man, it will be forgiven him; but to him who blasphemes against the Holy Spirit, it will not be forgiven. 11"Now when they bring you to the synagogues and magistrates and authorities, do not worry about how or what you should answer, or what you should say. 12For the Holy Spirit will teach you in that very hour what you ought to say."

THE PARABLE OF THE RICH FOOL

13Then one from the crowd said to Him, "Teacher, tell my brother to divide the inheritance with me."

14But He said to him, "Man, who made Me a judge or an arbitrator over you?" 15And He said to them, "Take heed and beware of covetousness,ᵃ for one's life does not consist in the abundance of the things he possesses."

11:54 ᵃ NU-Text omits *and seeking and that they might accuse Him.*   12:6 ᵃ Greek *assarion,* a coin of very small value   12:15 ᵃ NU-Text reads *all covetousness.*

LUKE 12:16

16Then He spoke a parable to them, saying: "The ground of a certain rich man yielded plentifully. 17And he thought within himself, saying, 'What shall I do, since I have no room to store my crops?' 18So he said, 'I will do this: I will pull down my barns and build greater, and there I will store all my crops and my goods. 19And I will say to my soul, "Soul, you have many goods laid up for many years; take your ease; eat, drink, *and be* merry." 20But God said to him, 'Fool! This night your soul will be required of you; then whose will those things be which you have provided?'

21"So *is* he who lays up treasure for himself, and is not rich toward God."

DO NOT WORRY

22Then He said to His disciples, "Therefore I say to you, do not worry about your life, what you will eat; nor about the body, what you will put on. 23Life is more than food, and the body *is* more than clothing. 24Consider the ravens, for they neither sow nor reap, which have neither storehouse nor barn; and God feeds them. Of how much more value are you than the birds? 25And which of you by worrying can add one cubit to his stature? 26If you then are not able to do *the* least, why are you anxious for the rest? 27Consider the lilies, how they grow: they neither toil nor spin; and yet I say to you, even Solomon in all his glory was not arrayed like one of these. ²⁸If then God so clothes the grass, which today is in the field and tomorrow is thrown into the oven, how much more *will He clothe* you, O you of little faith?

²⁹"And do not seek what you should eat or what you should drink, nor have an anxious mind. ³⁰For all these things the nations of the world seek after; and your Father knows that you need these things. ³¹But seek the kingdom of God, and all these things*ᵃ* shall be added to you.

³²"Do not fear, little flock, for it is your Father's good pleasure to give you the kingdom. ³³Sell what you have and give alms; provide yourselves money bags which do not grow old, a treasure in the heavens that does not fail, where no thief approaches nor moth destroys. ³⁴For where your treasure is, there your heart will be also.

THE FAITHFUL SERVANT AND THE EVIL SERVANT

³⁵"Let your waist be girded and *your* lamps burning; ³⁶and you yourselves be like men who wait for their master, when he will return from the wedding, that when he comes and knocks they may open to him immediately. ³⁷Blessed *are* those servants whom the master, when he comes, will find watching. Assuredly, I say to you that he will gird himself and have them sit down *to eat,* and will

12:31 *ᵃ* NU-Text reads *His kingdom, and these things.*

come and serve them. **38**And if he should come in the second watch, or come in the third watch, and find *them so*, blessed are those servants. **39**But know this, that if the master of the house had known what hour the thief would come, he would have watched and^a not allowed his house to be broken into. **40**Therefore you also be ready, for the Son of Man is coming at an hour you do not expect."

41Then Peter said to Him, "Lord, do You speak this parable *only* to us, or to all *people*?"

42And the Lord said, "Who then is that faithful and wise steward, whom *his* master will make ruler over his household, to give *them their* portion of food in due season? **43**Blessed *is* that servant whom his master will find so doing when he comes. **44**Truly, I say to you that he will make him ruler over all that he has. **45**But if that servant says in his heart, 'My master is delaying his coming,' and begins to beat the male and female servants, and to eat and drink and be drunk, **46**the master of that servant will come on a day when he is not looking for *him*, and at an hour when he is not aware, and will cut him in two and appoint *him* his portion with the unbelievers. **47**And that servant who knew his master's will, and did not prepare *himself* or do according to his will, shall be beaten with many *stripes*. **48**But he who did not know, yet committed things deserving of stripes, shall be beaten with few. For everyone to whom much is given, from him much will be required; and to whom much has been committed, of him they will ask the more.

CHRIST BRINGS DIVISION

49 "I came to send fire on the earth, and how I wish it were already kindled! 50 But I have a baptism to be baptized with, and how distressed I am till it is accomplished! 51 Do you suppose that I came to give peace on earth? I tell you, not at all, but rather division. 52 For from now on five in one house will be divided: three against two, and two against three. 53 Father will be divided against son and son against father, mother against daughter and daughter against mother, mother-in-law against her daughter-in-law and daughter-in-law against her mother-in-law."

DISCERN THE TIME

54 Then He also said to the multitudes, "Whenever you see a cloud rising out of the west, immediately you say, 'A shower is coming'; and so it is. 55 And when you see the south wind blow, you say, 'There will be hot weather'; and there is. 56 Hypocrites! You can discern the face of the sky and of the earth, but how is it you do not discern this time?

12:39 a NU-Text reads *he would not have allowed*.

LUKE 12:57

MAKE PEACE WITH YOUR ADVERSARY

57"Yes, and why, even of yourselves, do you not judge what is right? 58When you go with your adversary to the magistrate, make every effort along the way to settle with him, lest he drag you to the judge, the judge deliver you to the officer, and the officer throw you into prison. 59I tell you, you shall not depart from there till you have paid the very last mite."

REPENT OR PERISH

13 There were present at that season some who told Him about the Galileans whose blood Pilate had mingled with their sacrifices. 2And Jesus answered and said to them, "Do you suppose that these Galileans were worse sinners than all *other* Galileans, because they suffered such things? 3I tell you, no; but unless you repent you will all likewise perish. 4Or those eighteen on whom the tower in Siloam fell and killed them, do you think that they were worse sinners than all *other* men who dwelt in Jerusalem? 5I tell you, no; but unless you repent you will all likewise perish."

THE PARABLE OF THE BARREN FIG TREE

6He also spoke this parable: "A certain *man* had a fig tree planted in his vineyard, and he came seeking fruit on it and found none. [7]Then he said to the keeper of his vineyard, 'Look, for three years I have come seeking fruit on this fig tree and find none. Cut it down; why does it use up the ground?' [8]But he answered and said to him, 'Sir, let it alone this year also, until I dig around it and fertilize *it*. [9]And if it bears fruit, *well*. But if not, after that[a] you can cut it down.'"

A SPIRIT OF INFIRMITY

[10]Now He was teaching in one of the synagogues on the Sabbath. [11]And behold, there was a woman who had a spirit of infirmity eighteen years, and was bent over and could in no way raise *herself* up. [12]But when Jesus saw her, He called *her* to *Him* and said to her, "Woman, you are loosed from your infirmity." [13]And He laid *His* hands on her, and immediately she was made straight, and glorified God.

[14]But the ruler of the synagogue answered with indignation, because Jesus had healed on the Sabbath; and he said to the crowd, "There are six days on which men ought to work; therefore come and be healed on them, and not on the Sabbath day."

[15]The Lord then answered him and said, "Hypocrite![a] Does not each one of

13:9 [a] NU-Text reads *And if it bears fruit after that, well. But if not, you can cut it down.*   13:15 [a] NU-Text and M-Text read *Hypocrites.*

LUKE 13:16

you on the Sabbath loose his ox or donkey from the stall, and lead *it* away to water it? [16]So ought not this woman, being a daughter of Abraham, whom Satan has bound—think of it—for eighteen years, be loosed from this bond on the Sabbath?" [17]And when He said these things, all His adversaries were put to shame; and all the multitude rejoiced for all the glorious things that were done by Him.

THE PARABLE OF THE MUSTARD SEED

[18]Then He said, "What is the kingdom of God like? And to what shall I compare it? [19]It is like a mustard seed, which a man took and put in his garden; and it grew and became a large[a] tree, and the birds of the air nested in its branches."

THE PARABLE OF THE LEAVEN

[20]And again He said, "To what shall I liken the kingdom of God? [21]It is like leaven, which a woman took and hid in three measures[a] of meal till it was all leavened."

THE NARROW WAY

[22]And He went through the cities and villages, teaching, and journeying toward Jerusalem. [23]Then one said to Him, "Lord, are there few who are saved?"

And He said to them, [24]"Strive to enter through the narrow gate, for many, I say to you, will seek to enter and will not be able. [25]When once the Master of the house has risen up and shut the door, and you begin to stand outside and knock at the door, saying, 'Lord, Lord, open for us,' and He will answer and say to you, 'I do not know you, where you are from,' [26]then you will begin to say, 'We ate and drank in Your presence, and You taught in our streets.' [27]But He will say, 'I tell you I do not know you, where you are from. Depart from Me, all you workers of iniquity.' [28]There will be weeping and gnashing of teeth, when you see Abraham and Isaac and Jacob and all the prophets in the kingdom of God, and yourselves thrust out. [29]They will come from the east and the west, from the north and the south, and sit down in the kingdom of God. [30]And indeed there are last who will be first, and there are first who will be last."

[31]On that very day[a] some Pharisees came, saying to Him, "Get out and depart from here, for Herod wants to kill You."

[32]And He said to them, "Go, tell that fox, 'Behold, I cast out demons and perform cures today and tomorrow, and the third *day* I shall be perfected.' [33]Nevertheless I must journey today, tomorrow, and the *day* following; for it cannot be that a prophet should perish outside of Jerusalem.

13:19 [a] NU-Text omits *large*.   13:21 [a] Greek *sata*, approximately two pecks in all   13:31 [a] NU-Text reads *In that very hour.*

LUKE 13:34

JESUS LAMENTS OVER JERUSALEM

34"O Jerusalem, Jerusalem, the one who kills the prophets and stones those who are sent to her! How often I wanted to gather your children together, as a hen *gathers* her brood under *her* wings, but you were not willing! 35See! Your house is left to you desolate; and assuredly,ª I say to you, you shall not see Me until *the time* comes when you say, 'Blessed is He who comes in the name of the LORD!'"b

A MAN WITH DROPSY HEALED ON THE SABBATH

14 Now it happened, as He went into the house of one of the rulers of the Pharisees to eat bread on the Sabbath, that they watched Him closely. 2And behold, there was a certain man before Him who had dropsy. 3And Jesus, answering, spoke to the lawyers and Pharisees, saying, "Is it lawful to heal on the Sabbath?"ª

4But they kept silent. And He took *him* and healed him, and let him go. 5Then He answered them, saying, "Which of you, having a donkeyª or an ox that has fallen into a pit, will not immediately pull him out on the Sabbath day?" 6And they could not answer Him regarding these things.

TAKE THE LOWLY PLACE

7So He told a parable to those who were invited, when He noted how they chose the best places, saying to them: [8]"When you are invited by anyone to a wedding feast, do not sit down in the best place, lest one more honorable than you be invited by him; [9]and he who invited you and him come and say to you, 'Give place to this man,' and then you begin with shame to take the lowest place. [10]But when you are invited, go and sit down in the lowest place, so that when he who invited you comes he may say to you, 'Friend, go up higher.' Then you will have glory in the presence of those who sit at the table with you. [11]For whoever exalts himself will be humbled, and he who humbles himself will be exalted."

[12]Then He also said to him who invited Him, "When you give a dinner or a supper, do not ask your friends, your brothers, your relatives, nor rich neighbors, lest they also invite you back, and you be repaid. [13]But when you give a feast, invite *the poor, the* maimed, *the* lame, *the* blind. [14]And you will be blessed, because they cannot repay you; for you shall be repaid at the resurrection of the just."

THE PARABLE OF THE GREAT SUPPER

[15]Now when one of those who sat at the table with Him heard these things, he said to Him, "Blessed *is* he who shall eat bread[a] in the kingdom of God!"

[16]Then He said to him, "A certain man gave a great supper and invited many,

13:35 [a] NU-Text and M-Text omit *assuredly.*   [b] Psalm 118:26   14:3 [a] NU-Text adds *or not.*
14:5 [a] NU-Text and M-Text read *son.*   14:15 [a] M-Text reads *dinner.*

LUKE 14:17

17and sent his servant at supper time to say to those who were invited, 'Come, for all things are now ready.' 18But they all with one *accord* began to make excuses. The first said to him, 'I have bought a piece of ground, and I must go and see it. I ask you to have me excused.' 19And another said, 'I have bought five yoke of oxen, and I am going to test them. I ask you to have me excused.' 20Still another said, 'I have married a wife, and therefore I cannot come.' 21So that servant came and reported these things to his master. Then the master of the house, being angry, said to his servant, 'Go out quickly into the streets and lanes of the city, and bring in here *the* poor and *the* maimed and *the* lame and *the* blind.' 22And the servant said, 'Master, it is done as you commanded, and still there is room.' 23Then the master said to the servant, 'Go out into the highways and hedges, and compel *them* to come in, that my house may be filled. 24For I say to you that none of those men who were invited shall taste my supper.'"

LEAVING ALL TO FOLLOW CHRIST

25Now great multitudes went with Him. And He turned and said to them, 26"If anyone comes to Me and does not hate his father and mother, wife and children, brothers and sisters, yes, and his own life also, he cannot be My disciple. 27And whoever does not bear his cross and come after Me cannot be My disciple. **28**For which of you, intending to build a tower, does not sit down first and count the cost, whether he has *enough* to finish *it* — **29**lest, after he has laid the foundation, and is not able to finish, all who see *it* begin to mock him, **30**saying, 'This man began to build and was not able to finish'? **31**Or what king, going to make war against another king, does not sit down first and consider whether he is able with ten thousand to meet him who comes against him with twenty thousand? **32**Or else, while the other is still a great way off, he sends a delegation and asks conditions of peace. **33**So likewise, whoever of you does not forsake all that he has cannot be My disciple.

TASTELESS SALT IS WORTHLESS

34"Salt *is* good; but if the salt has lost its flavor, how shall it be seasoned? **35**It is neither fit for the land nor for the dunghill, *but* men throw it out. He who has ears to hear, let him hear!"

THE PARABLE OF THE LOST SHEEP

15 Then all the tax collectors and the sinners drew near to Him to hear Him. **2**And the Pharisees and scribes complained, saying, "This Man receives sinners and eats with them." **3**So He spoke this parable to them, saying:

4"What man of you, having a hundred sheep, if he loses one of them, does not leave the ninety-nine in the wilderness, and go after the one which is lost until he finds it? [5] And when he has found it, he lays it on his shoulders, rejoicing. [6] And when he comes home, he calls together his friends and neighbors, saying to them, 'Rejoice with me, for I have found my sheep which was lost!' [7] I say to you that likewise there will be more joy in heaven over one sinner who repents than over ninety-nine just persons who need no repentance.

THE PARABLE OF THE LOST COIN

[8] "Or what woman, having ten silver coins, [a] if she loses one coin, does not light a lamp, sweep the house, and search carefully until she finds it? [9] And when she has found it, she calls her friends and neighbors together, saying, 'Rejoice with me, for I have found the piece which I lost!' [10] Likewise, I say to you, there is joy in the presence of the angels of God over one sinner who repents."

THE PARABLE OF THE LOST SON

[11] Then He said: "A certain man had two sons. [12] And the younger of them said to his father, 'Father, give me the portion of goods that falls to me.' So he divided to them his livelihood. [13] And not many days after, the younger son gathered all together, journeyed to a far country, and there wasted his possessions with

prodigal living. **14**But when he had spent all, there arose a severe famine in that land, and he began to be in want. **15**Then he went and joined himself to a citizen of that country, and he sent him into his fields to feed swine. **16**And he would gladly have filled his stomach with the pods that the swine ate, and no one gave him *anything.*

17"But when he came to himself, he said, 'How many of my father's hired servants have bread enough and to spare, and I perish with hunger! **18**I will arise and go to my father, and will say to him, "Father, I have sinned against heaven and before you, **19**and I am no longer worthy to be called your son. Make me like one of your hired servants.'"

20"And he arose and came to his father. But when he was still a great way off, his father saw him and had compassion, and ran and fell on his neck and kissed him. **21**And the son said to him, 'Father, I have sinned against heaven and in your sight, and am no longer worthy to be called your son.'

22"But the father said to his servants, 'Bring*ᵃ* out the best robe and put *it* on him, and put a ring on his hand and sandals on *his* feet. **23**And bring the fatted calf here and kill *it,* and let us eat and be merry; **24**for this my son was dead and is alive again; he was lost and is found.' And they began to be merry.

15:8 *ᵃ* Greek *drachma,* a valuable coin often worn in a ten-piece garland by married women
15:22 *ᵃ* NU-Text reads *Quickly bring.*

25"Now his older son was in the field. And as he came and drew near to the house, he heard music and dancing. 26So he called one of the servants and asked what these things meant. 27And he said to him, 'Your brother has come, and because he has received him safe and sound, your father has killed the fatted calf.'

28"But he was angry and would not go in. Therefore his father came out and pleaded with him. 29So he answered and said to *his* father, 'Lo, these many years I have been serving you; I never transgressed your commandment at any time; and yet you never gave me a young goat, that I might make merry with my friends. 30But as soon as this son of yours came, who has devoured your livelihood with harlots, you killed the fatted calf for him.'

31"And he said to him, 'Son, you are always with me, and all that I have is yours. 32It was right that we should make merry and be glad, for your brother was dead and is alive again, and was lost and is found.'"

THE PARABLE OF THE UNJUST STEWARD

16 He also said to His disciples: "There was a certain rich man who had a steward, and an accusation was brought to him that this man was wasting his goods. 2So he called him and said to him, 'What is this I hear about you? Give an account of your stewardship, for you can no longer be steward.'

3 "Then the steward said within himself, 'What shall I do? For my master is taking the stewardship away from me. I cannot dig; I am ashamed to beg. 4 I have resolved what to do, that when I am put out of the stewardship, they may receive me into their houses.'

5 "So he called every one of his master's debtors to *him*, and said to the first, 'How much do you owe my master?' 6 And he said, 'A hundred measures[a] of oil.' So he said to him, 'Take your bill, and sit down quickly and write fifty.' 7 Then he said to another, 'And how much do you owe?' So he said, 'A hundred measures[a] of wheat.' And he said to him, 'Take your bill, and write eighty.' 8 So the master commended the unjust steward because he had dealt shrewdly. For the sons of this world are more shrewd in their generation than the sons of light.

9 "And I say to you, make friends for yourselves by unrighteous mammon, that when you fail,[a] they may receive you into an everlasting home. 10 He who is faithful in *what is* least is faithful also in much; and he who is unjust in *what is* least is unjust also in much. 11 Therefore if you have not been faithful in the unrighteous mammon, who will commit to your trust the true *riches?* 12 And if you have not been faithful in what is another man's, who will give you what is your own?

16:6 [a] Greek *batos*, eight or nine gallons each (Old Testament *bath*)   16:7 [a] Greek *koros*, ten or twelve bushels each (Old Testament *kor*)   16:9 [a] NU-Text reads it fails.

LUKE 16:13

13"No servant can serve two masters; for either he will hate the one and love the other, or else he will be loyal to the one and despise the other. You cannot serve God and mammon."

THE LAW, THE PROPHETS, AND THE KINGDOM

14Now the Pharisees, who were lovers of money, also heard all these things, and they derided Him. 15And He said to them, "You are those who justify yourselves before men, but God knows your hearts. For what is highly esteemed among men is an abomination in the sight of God.

16"The law and the prophets *were* until John. Since that time the kingdom of God has been preached, and everyone is pressing into it. 17And it is easier for heaven and earth to pass away than for one tittle of the law to fail.

18"Whoever divorces his wife and marries another commits adultery; and whoever marries her who is divorced from *her* husband commits adultery.

THE RICH MAN AND LAZARUS

19"There was a certain rich man who was clothed in purple and fine linen and fared sumptuously every day. 20But there was a certain beggar named Lazarus, full of sores, who was laid at his gate, 21desiring to be fed with the crumbs which fell[a] from the rich man's table. Moreover the dogs came and licked his sores. 22So it was that the beggar died, and was carried by the angels to Abraham's bosom. The rich man also died and was buried. 23And being in torments in Hades, he lifted up his eyes and saw Abraham afar off, and Lazarus in his bosom.

24"Then he cried and said, 'Father Abraham, have mercy on me, and send Lazarus that he may dip the tip of his finger in water and cool my tongue; for I am tormented in this flame.' 25But Abraham said, 'Son, remember that in your lifetime you received your good things, and likewise Lazarus evil things; but now he is comforted and you are tormented. 26And besides all this, between us and you there is a great gulf fixed, so that those who want to pass from here to you cannot, nor can those from there pass to us.'

27"Then he said, 'I beg you therefore, father, that you would send him to my father's house, 28for I have five brothers, that he may testify to them, lest they also come to this place of torment.' 29Abraham said to him, 'They have Moses and the prophets; let them hear them.' 30And he said, 'No, father Abraham; but if one goes to them from the dead, they will repent.' 31But he said to him, 'If they do not hear Moses and the prophets, neither will they be persuaded though one rise from the dead.' "

16:21 [a] NU-Text reads *with what fell.*

LUKE 17:1

JESUS WARNS OF OFFENSES

17 Then He said to the disciples, "It is impossible that no offenses should come, but woe *to him* through whom they do come! [2]It would be better for him if a millstone were hung around his neck, and he were thrown into the sea, than that he should offend one of these little ones. [3]Take heed to yourselves. If your brother sins against you,[a] rebuke him; and if he repents, forgive him. [4]And if he sins against you seven times in a day, and seven times in a day returns to you,[a] saying, 'I repent,' you shall forgive him."

FAITH AND DUTY

[5]And the apostles said to the Lord, "Increase our faith."

[6]So the Lord said, "If you have faith as a mustard seed, you can say to this mulberry tree, 'Be pulled up by the roots and be planted in the sea,' and it would obey you. [7]And which of you, having a servant plowing or tending sheep, will say to him when he has come in from the field, 'Come at once and sit down to eat'? [8]But will he not rather say to him, 'Prepare something for my supper, and gird yourself and serve me till I have eaten and drunk, and afterward you will eat and drink'? [9]Does he thank that servant because he did the things that were commanded him? I think not.[a] [10]So likewise you, when you have done all those

things which you are commanded, say, 'We are unprofitable servants. We have done what was our duty to do.'"

TEN LEPERS CLEANSED

11Now it happened as He went to Jerusalem that He passed through the midst of Samaria and Galilee. 12Then as He entered a certain village, there met Him ten men who were lepers, who stood afar off. 13And they lifted up *their* voices and said, "Jesus, Master, have mercy on us!"

14So when He saw *them*, He said to them, "Go, show yourselves to the priests." And so it was that as they went, they were cleansed.

15And one of them, when he saw that he was healed, returned, and with a loud voice glorified God, 16and fell down on *his* face at His feet, giving Him thanks. And he was a Samaritan.

17So Jesus answered and said, "Were there not ten cleansed? But where *are* the nine? 18Were there not any found who returned to give glory to God except this foreigner?" 19And He said to him, "Arise, go your way. Your faith has made you well."

17:3 *a* NU-Text omits *against you.*   17:4 *a* NU-Text omits *to you.*   17:9 *a* NU-Text ends verse with *commanded;* M-Text omits *him.*

LUKE 17:20

THE COMING OF THE KINGDOM

20Now when He was asked by the Pharisees when the kingdom of God would come, He answered them and said, "The kingdom of God does not come with observation; 21nor will they say, 'See here!' or 'See there!'[a] For indeed, the kingdom of God is within you."

22Then He said to the disciples, "The days will come when you will desire to see one of the days of the Son of Man, and you will not see *it.* 23And they will say to you, 'Look here!' or 'Look there!'[a] Do not go after *them* or follow *them.* 24For as the lightning that flashes out of one *part* under heaven shines to the other *part* under heaven, so also the Son of Man will be in His day. 25But first He must suffer many things and be rejected by this generation. 26And as it was in the days of Noah, so it will be also in the days of the Son of Man: 27They ate, they drank, they married wives, they were given in marriage, until the day that Noah entered the ark, and the flood came and destroyed them all. 28Likewise as it was also in the days of Lot: They ate, they drank, they bought, they sold, they planted, they built; 29but on the day that Lot went out of Sodom it rained fire and brimstone from heaven and destroyed *them* all. 30Even so will it be in the day when the Son of Man is revealed.

31"In that day, he who is on the housetop, and his goods *are* in the house, let him not come down to take them away. And likewise the one who is in the field, let him not turn back. 32Remember Lot's wife. 33Whoever seeks to save his life will lose it, and whoever loses his life will preserve it. 34I tell you, in that night there will be two *men* in one bed: the one will be taken and the other will be left. 35Two *women* will be grinding together: the one will be taken and the other left. 36Two *men* will be in the field: the one will be taken and the other left."[a]

37And they answered and said to Him, "Where, Lord?"

So He said to them, "Wherever the body is, there the eagles will be gathered together."

THE PARABLE OF THE PERSISTENT WIDOW

18 Then He spoke a parable to them, that men always ought to pray and not lose heart, 2saying: "There was in a certain city a judge who did not fear God nor regard man. 3Now there was a widow in that city; and she came to him, saying, 'Get justice for me from my adversary.' 4And he would not for a while; but afterward he said within himself, 'Though I do not fear God nor regard man, 5yet because this widow troubles me I will avenge her, lest by her continual coming she weary me.'"

17:21 [a] NU-Text reverses *here* and *there.*   17:23 [a] NU-Text reverses *here* and *there.*   17:36 [a] NU-Text and M-Text omit verse 36.

⁶Then the Lord said, "Hear what the unjust judge said. ⁷And shall God not avenge His own elect who cry out day and night to Him, though He bears long with them? ⁸I tell you that He will avenge them speedily. Nevertheless, when the Son of Man comes, will He really find faith on the earth?"

THE PARABLE OF THE PHARISEE AND THE TAX COLLECTOR

⁹Also He spoke this parable to some who trusted in themselves that they were righteous, and despised others: ¹⁰"Two men went up to the temple to pray, one a Pharisee and the other a tax collector. ¹¹The Pharisee stood and prayed thus with himself, 'God, I thank You that I am not like other men—extortioners, unjust, adulterers, or even as this tax collector. ¹²I fast twice a week; I give tithes of all that I possess.' ¹³And the tax collector, standing afar off, would not so much as raise *his* eyes to heaven, but beat his breast, saying, 'God, be merciful to me a sinner!' ¹⁴I tell you, this man went down to his house justified *rather* than the other; for everyone who exalts himself will be humbled, and he who humbles himself will be exalted."

JESUS BLESSES LITTLE CHILDREN

¹⁵Then they also brought infants to Him that He might touch them; but

when the disciples saw *it*, they rebuked them. ¹⁶But Jesus called them to *Him* and said, "Let the little children come to Me, and do not forbid them; for of such is the kingdom of God. ¹⁷Assuredly, I say to you, whoever does not receive the kingdom of God as a little child will by no means enter it."

JESUS COUNSELS THE RICH YOUNG RULER

¹⁸Now a certain ruler asked Him, saying, "Good Teacher, what shall I do to inherit eternal life?"

¹⁹So Jesus said to him, "Why do you call Me good? No one *is* good but One, *that is*, God. ²⁰You know the commandments: 'Do not commit adultery,' 'Do not murder,' 'Do not steal,' 'Do not bear false witness,' 'Honor your father and your mother.'"ᵃ

²¹And he said, "All these things I have kept from my youth."

²²So when Jesus heard these things, He said to him, "You still lack one thing. Sell all that you have and distribute to the poor, and you will have treasure in heaven; and come, follow Me."

²³But when he heard this, he became very sorrowful, for he was very rich.

18:20 ᵃ Exodus 20:12–16; Deuteronomy 5:16–20

WITH GOD ALL THINGS ARE POSSIBLE

²⁴And when Jesus saw that he became very sorrowful, He said, "How hard it is for those who have riches to enter the kingdom of God! ²⁵For it is easier for a camel to go through the eye of a needle than for a rich man to enter the kingdom of God."

²⁶And those who heard it said, "Who then can be saved?"

²⁷But He said, "The things which are impossible with men are possible with God."

²⁸Then Peter said, "See, we have left all[a] and followed You."

²⁹So He said to them, "Assuredly, I say to you, there is no one who has left house or parents or brothers or wife or children, for the sake of the kingdom of God, ³⁰who shall not receive many times more in this present time, and in the age to come eternal life."

JESUS A THIRD TIME PREDICTS HIS DEATH AND RESURRECTION

³¹Then He took the twelve aside and said to them, "Behold, we are going up to Jerusalem, and all things that are written by the prophets concerning the Son of Man will be accomplished. ³²For He will be delivered to the Gentiles and will

be mocked and insulted and spit upon. 33They will scourge *Him* and kill Him. And the third day He will rise again."

34But they understood none of these things; this saying was hidden from them, and they did not know the things which were spoken.

A BLIND MAN RECEIVES HIS SIGHT

35Then it happened, as He was coming near Jericho, that a certain blind man sat by the road begging. 36And hearing a multitude passing by, he asked what it meant. 37So they told him that Jesus of Nazareth was passing by. 38And he cried out, saying, "Jesus, Son of David, have mercy on me!"

39Then those who went before warned him that he should be quiet; but he cried out all the more, "Son of David, have mercy on me!"

40So Jesus stood still and commanded him to be brought to Him. And when he had come near, He asked him, 41saying, "What do you want Me to do for you?"

He said, "Lord, that I may receive my sight."

42Then Jesus said to him, "Receive your sight; your faith has made you well." 43And immediately he received his sight, and followed Him, glorifying God. And all the people, when they saw *it*, gave praise to God.

18:28 *a* NU-Text reads *our own.*

94

LUKE 19:1

JESUS COMES TO ZACCHAEUS' HOUSE

19 ¹ Then *Jesus* entered and passed through Jericho. ²Now behold, *there was* a man named Zacchaeus who was a chief tax collector, and he was rich. ³And he sought to see who Jesus was, but could not because of the crowd, for he was of short stature. ⁴So he ran ahead and climbed up into a sycamore tree to see Him, for He was going to pass that *way.* ⁵And when Jesus came to the place, He looked up and saw him,ᵃ and said to him, "Zacchaeus, make haste and come down, for today I must stay at your house." ⁶So he made haste and came down, and received Him joyfully. ⁷But when they saw *it,* they all complained, saying, "He has gone to be a guest with a man who is a sinner."

⁸Then Zacchaeus stood and said to the Lord, "Look, Lord, I give half of my goods to the poor; and if I have taken anything from anyone by false accusation, I restore fourfold."

⁹And Jesus said to him, "Today salvation has come to this house, because he also is a son of Abraham; ¹⁰for the Son of Man has come to seek and to save that which was lost."

THE PARABLE OF THE MINAS

¹¹Now as they heard these things, He spoke another parable, because He was

near Jerusalem and because they thought the kingdom of God would appear immediately. [12]Therefore He said: "A certain nobleman went into a far country to receive for himself a kingdom and to return. [13]So he called ten of his servants, delivered to them ten minas,[a] and said to them, 'Do business till I come.' [14]But his citizens hated him, and sent a delegation after him, saying, 'We will not have this *man* to reign over us.'

[15]"And so it was that when he returned, having received the kingdom, he then commanded these servants, to whom he had given the money, to be called to him, that he might know how much every man had gained by trading. [16]Then came the first, saying, 'Master, your mina has earned ten minas.' [17]And he said to him, 'Well *done*, good servant; because you were faithful in a very little, have authority over ten cities.' [18]And the second came, saying, 'Master, your mina has earned five minas.' [19]Likewise he said to him, 'You also be over five cities.'

[20]"Then another came, saying, 'Master, here is your mina, which I have kept put away in a handkerchief. [21]For I feared you, because you are an austere man. You collect what you did not deposit, and reap what you did not sow.' [22]And he said to him, 'Out of your own mouth I will judge you, *you* wicked servant. You knew that I was an austere man, collecting what I did not deposit and reaping

19:5 [a] NU-Text omits *and saw him.* 19:13 [a] The *mina* (Greek *mna*, Hebrew *minah*) was worth about three months' salary.

what I did not sow. 23Why then did you not put my money in the bank, that at my coming I might have collected it with interest?'

24"And he said to those who stood by, 'Take the mina from him, and give *it* to him who has ten minas.' 25(But they said to him, 'Master, he has ten minas.') 26'For I say to you, that to everyone who has will be given; and from him who does not have, even what he has will be taken away from him. 27But bring here those enemies of mine, who did not want me to reign over them, and slay *them* before me.'"

THE TRIUMPHAL ENTRY

28When He had said this, He went on ahead, going up to Jerusalem. 29And it came to pass, when He drew near to Bethphage^a and Bethany, at the mountain called Olivet, *that* He sent two of His disciples, 30saying, "Go into the village opposite *you*, where as you enter *you* will find a colt tied, on which no one has ever sat. Loose it and bring *it here*. 31And if anyone asks you, 'Why are you loosing *it?*' thus you shall say to him, 'Because the Lord has need of it.'"

32So those who were sent went their way and found *it* just as He had said to them. 33But as they were loosing the colt, the owners of it said to them, "Why are you loosing the colt?"

34And they said, "The Lord has need of him." 35Then they brought him to Jesus. And they threw their own clothes on the colt, and they set Jesus on him. 36And as He went, *many* spread their clothes on the road.

37Then, as He was now drawing near the descent of the Mount of Olives, the whole multitude of the disciples began to rejoice and praise God with a loud voice for all the mighty works they had seen, 38saying:

"'Blessed *is* the King who comes in the name of the LORD!'[a]
Peace in heaven and glory in the highest!"

39And some of the Pharisees called to Him from the crowd, "Teacher, rebuke Your disciples."

40But He answered and said to them, "I tell you that if these should keep silent, the stones would immediately cry out."

JESUS WEEPS OVER JERUSALEM

41Now as He drew near, He saw the city and wept over it, 42saying, "If you had known, even you, especially in this your day, the things *that make* for your peace! But now they are hidden from your eyes. 43For days will come upon you

19:29 [a] M-Text reads *Bethsphage*.   19:38 [a] Psalm 118:26

when your enemies will build an embankment around you, surround you and close you in on every side, ⁴⁴and level you, and your children within you, to the ground; and they will not leave in you one stone upon another, because you did not know the time of your visitation."

JESUS CLEANSES THE TEMPLE

⁴⁵Then He went into the temple and began to drive out those who bought and sold in it,ᵃ ⁴⁶saying to them, "It is written, 'My house isᵃ a house of prayer,'ᵇ but you have made it a 'den of thieves.'"ᶜ

⁴⁷And He was teaching daily in the temple. But the chief priests, the scribes, and the leaders of the people sought to destroy Him, ⁴⁸and were unable to do anything; for all the people were very attentive to hear Him.

JESUS' AUTHORITY QUESTIONED

20 Now it happened on one of those days, as He taught the people in the temple and preached the gospel, *that* the chief priests and the scribes, together with the elders, confronted *Him* ²and spoke to Him, saying, "Tell us, by what authority are You doing these things? Or who is he who gave You this authority?"

[3]But He answered and said to them, "I also will ask you one thing, and answer Me: [4]The baptism of John—was it from heaven or from men?"

[5]And they reasoned among themselves, saying, "If we say, 'From heaven,' He will say, 'Why then[a] did you not believe him?' [6]But if we say, 'From men,' all the people will stone us, for they are persuaded that John was a prophet." [7]So they answered that they did not know where *it was* from.

[8]And Jesus said to them, "Neither will I tell you by what authority I do these things."

THE PARABLE OF THE WICKED VINEDRESSERS

[9]Then He began to tell the people this parable: "A certain man planted a vineyard, leased it to vinedressers, and went into a far country for a long time. [10]Now at vintage-time he sent a servant to the vinedressers, that they might give him some of the fruit of the vineyard. But the vinedressers beat him and sent *him* away empty-handed. [11]Again he sent another servant; and they beat him also, treated *him* shamefully, and sent *him* away empty-handed. [12]And again he sent a third; and they wounded him also and cast *him* out.

[13]"Then the owner of the vineyard said, 'What shall I do? I will send my

19:45 [a] NU-Text reads *those who were selling.*   19:46 [a] NU-Text reads *shall be.*   [b] Isaiah 56:7   [c] Jeremiah
7:11   20:5 [a] NU-Text and M-Text omit *then.*

beloved son. Probably they will respect *him* when they see him.' **14**But when the vinedressers saw him, they reasoned among themselves, saying, "This is the heir. Come, let us kill him, that the inheritance may be ours.' **15**So they cast him out of the vineyard and killed *him*. Therefore what will the owner of the vineyard do to them? **16**He will come and destroy those vinedressers and give the vineyard to others."

And when they heard *it* they said, "Certainly not!"

17Then He looked at them and said, "What then is this that is written:

'The stone which the builders rejected
Has become the chief cornerstone'?ᵃ

18Whoever falls on that stone will be broken; but on whomever it falls, it will grind him to powder."

19And the chief priests and the scribes that very hour sought to lay hands on Him, but they feared the peopleᵃ—for they knew He had spoken this parable against them.

THE PHARISEES: IS IT LAWFUL TO PAY TAXES TO CAESAR?

20 So they watched *Him*, and sent spies who pretended to be righteous, that they might seize on His words, in order to deliver Him to the power and the authority of the governor.

21 Then they asked Him, saying, "Teacher, we know that You say and teach rightly, and You do not show personal favoritism, but teach the way of God in truth: 22 Is it lawful for us to pay taxes to Caesar or not?"

23 But He perceived their craftiness, and said to them, "Why do you test Me?[a] 24 Show Me a denarius. Whose image and inscription does it have?"

They answered and said, "Caesar's."

25 And He said to them, "Render therefore to Caesar the things that are Caesar's, and to God the things that are God's."

26 But they could not catch Him in His words in the presence of the people. And they marveled at His answer and kept silent.

THE SADDUCEES: WHAT ABOUT THE RESURRECTION?

27 Then some of the Sadducees, who deny that there is a resurrection, came to *Him* and asked Him, 28 saying: "Teacher, Moses wrote to us *that* if a man's

20:17 [a] Psalm 118:22   20:19 [a] M-Text reads *but they were afraid.*   20:23 [a] NU-Text omits *why do you test Me?*

brother dies, having a wife, and he dies without children, his brother should take his wife and raise up offspring for his brother. ²⁹Now there were seven brothers. And the first took a wife, and died without children. ³⁰And the second^a took her as wife, and he died childless. ³¹Then the third took her, and in like manner the seven also; and they left no children,^a and died. ³²Last of all the woman died also. ³³Therefore, in the resurrection, whose wife does she become? For all seven had her as wife."

³⁴Jesus answered and said to them, "The sons of this age marry and are given in marriage. ³⁵But those who are counted worthy to attain that age, and the resurrection from the dead, neither marry nor are given in marriage; ³⁶nor can they die anymore, for they are equal to the angels and are sons of God, being sons of the resurrection. ³⁷But even Moses showed in the *burning bush passage* that the dead are raised, when he called the Lord 'the God of Abraham, the God of Isaac, and the God of Jacob.'^a ³⁸For He is not the God of the dead but of the living, for all live to Him."

³⁹Then some of the scribes answered and said, "Teacher, You have spoken well." ⁴⁰But after that they dared not question Him anymore.

means pass away till all things take place. 33Heaven and earth will pass away, but My words will by no means pass away.

THE IMPORTANCE OF WATCHING

34"But take heed to yourselves, lest your hearts be weighed down with carousing, drunkenness, and cares of this life, and that Day come on you unexpectedly. 35For it will come as a snare on all those who dwell on the face of the whole earth. 36Watch therefore, and pray always that you may be counted worthy[a] to escape all these things that will come to pass, and to stand before the Son of Man."

37And in the daytime He was teaching in the temple, but at night He went out and stayed on the mountain called Olivet. 38Then early in the morning all the people came to Him in the temple to hear Him.

THE PLOT TO KILL JESUS

22 Now the Feast of Unleavened Bread drew near, which is called Passover. 2And the chief priests and the scribes sought how they might kill Him, for they feared the people.

3Then Satan entered Judas, surnamed Iscariot, who was numbered among the twelve. 4So he went his way and conferred with the chief priests and captains,

21:36 a NU-Text reads may have strength.

how he might betray Him to them. 5 And they were glad, and agreed to give him money. 6 So he promised and sought opportunity to betray Him to them in the absence of the multitude.

JESUS AND HIS DISCIPLES PREPARE THE PASSOVER

7 Then came the Day of Unleavened Bread, when the Passover must be killed. 8 And He sent Peter and John, saying, "Go and prepare the Passover for us, that we may eat."

9 So they said to Him, "Where do You want us to prepare?"

10 And He said to them, "Behold, when you have entered the city, a man will meet you carrying a pitcher of water; follow him into the house which he enters. 11 Then you shall say to the master of the house, 'The Teacher says to you, "Where is the guest room where I may eat the Passover with My disciples?" ' 12 Then he will show you a large, furnished upper room; there make ready."

13 So they went and found it just as He had said to them, and they prepared the Passover.

JESUS INSTITUTES THE LORD'S SUPPER

14 When the hour had come, He sat down, and the twelve[a] apostles with Him.

PETER DENIES JESUS, AND WEEPS BITTERLY

⁵⁴Having arrested Him, they led *Him* and brought Him into the high priest's house. But Peter followed at a distance. ⁵⁵Now when they had kindled a fire in the midst of the courtyard and sat down together, Peter sat among them. ⁵⁶And a certain servant girl, seeing him as he sat by the fire, looked intently at him and said, "This man was also with Him."

⁵⁷But he denied Him,ᵃ saying, "Woman, I do not know Him."

⁵⁸And after a little while another saw him and said, "You also are of them." But Peter said, "Man, I am not!"

⁵⁹Then after about an hour had passed, another confidently affirmed, saying, "Surely this *fellow* also was with Him, for he is a Galilean."

⁶⁰But Peter said, "Man, I do not know what you are saying!"

Immediately, while he was still speaking, the roosterᵃ crowed. ⁶¹And the Lord turned and looked at Peter. Then Peter remembered the word of the Lord, how He had said to him, "Before the rooster crows,ᵃ you will deny Me three times."

⁶²So Peter went out and wept bitterly.

22:44 ᵃ NU-Text brackets verses 43 and 44 as not in the original text.   22:57 ᵃ NU-Text reads *denied it*.
22:60 ᵃ NU-Text and M-Text read *a rooster*.   22:61 ᵃ NU-Text adds *today*.

LUKE 22:63

JESUS MOCKED AND BEATEN

63Now the men who held Jesus mocked Him and beat Him. 64And having blindfolded Him, they struck Him on the face and asked Him,ª saying, "Prophesy! Who is the one who struck You?" 65And many other things they blasphemously spoke against Him.

JESUS FACES THE SANHEDRIN

66As soon as it was day, the elders of the people, both chief priests and scribes, came together and led Him into their council, saying, 67"If You are the Christ, tell us."

But He said to them, "If I tell you, you will by no means believe. 68And if I also ask *you*, you will by no means answer Me or let *Me* go.ª 69Hereafter the Son of Man will sit on the right hand of the power of God."

70Then they all said, "Are You then the Son of God?"

So He said to them, "You *rightly* say that I am."

71And they said, "What further testimony do we need? For we have heard it ourselves from His own mouth."

JESUS HANDED OVER TO PONTIUS PILATE

23 Then the whole multitude of them arose and led Him to Pilate. 2 And they began to accuse Him, saying, "We found this *fellow* perverting the ͣ nation, and forbidding to pay taxes to Caesar, saying that He Himself is Christ, a King."

3 Then Pilate asked Him, saying, "Are You the King of the Jews?"

He answered him and said, "*It is as you say.*"

4 So Pilate said to the chief priests and the crowd, "I find no fault in this Man."

5 But they were the more fierce, saying, "He stirs up the people, teaching throughout all Judea, beginning from Galilee to this place."

JESUS FACES HEROD

6 When Pilate heard of Galilee, ͣ he asked if the Man were a Galilean. 7 And as soon as he knew that He belonged to Herod's jurisdiction, he sent Him to Herod, who was also in Jerusalem at that time. 8 Now when Herod saw Jesus, he was exceedingly glad; for he had desired for a long *time* to see Him, because he had heard many things about Him, and he hoped to see some miracle done by Him. 9 Then he questioned Him with many words, but He answered him nothing. 10 And the chief priests and scribes stood and vehemently accused Him.

22:64 ͣ NU-Text reads *And having blindfolded Him, they asked Him.*   22:68 ͣ NU-Text omits *also* and *Me or let Me go.*   23:2 ͣ NU-Text reads *our.*   23:6 ͣ NU-Text omits *of Galilee.*

LUKE 23:11

¹¹Then Herod, with his men of war, treated Him with contempt and mocked *Him*, arrayed Him in a gorgeous robe, and sent Him back to Pilate. ¹²That very day Pilate and Herod became friends with each other, for previously they had been at enmity with each other.

TAKING THE PLACE OF BARABBAS

¹³Then Pilate, when he had called together the chief priests, the rulers, and the people, ¹⁴said to them, "You have brought this Man to me, as one who misleads the people. And indeed, having examined *Him* in your presence, I have found no fault in this Man concerning those things of which you accuse Him; ¹⁵no, neither did Herod, for I sent you back to him;ᵃ and indeed nothing deserving of death has been done by Him. ¹⁶I will therefore chastise Him and release *Him* ¹⁷(for it was necessary for him to release one to them at the feast).ᵃ

¹⁸And they all cried out at once, saying, "Away with this *Man*, and release to us Barabbas" — ¹⁹who had been thrown into prison for a certain rebellion made in the city, and for murder.

²⁰Pilate, therefore, wishing to release Jesus, again called out to them. ²¹But they shouted, saying, "Crucify *Him*, crucify *Him*!"

²²Then he said to them the third time, "Why, what evil has He done? I have

by them in shining garments. ⁵Then, as they were afraid and bowed *their* faces to the earth, they said to them, "Why do you seek the living among the dead? ⁶He is not here, but is risen! Remember how He spoke to you when He was still in Galilee, ⁷saying, 'The Son of Man must be delivered into the hands of sinful men, and be crucified, and the third day rise again.'"

⁸And they remembered His words. ⁹Then they returned from the tomb and told all these things to the eleven and to all the rest. ¹⁰It was Mary Magdalene, Joanna, Mary *the mother* of James, and the other *women* with them, who told these things to the apostles. ¹¹And their words seemed to them like idle tales, and they did not believe them. ¹²But Peter arose and ran to the tomb; and stooping down, he saw the linen cloths lying*ᵃ* by themselves; and he departed, marveling to himself at what had happened.

THE ROAD TO EMMAUS

¹³Now behold, two of them were traveling that same day to a village called Emmaus, which was seven miles*ᵃ* from Jerusalem. ¹⁴And they talked together of all these things which had happened. ¹⁵So it was, while they conversed and

23:51 *ᵃ* NU-Text reads *who was waiting.*   24:1 *ᵃ* NU-Text omits *and certain other women with them.*
24:4 *ᵃ* NU-Text omits *greatly.*   24:12 *ᵃ* NU-Text omits *lying.*   24:13 *ᵃ* Literally *sixty stadia*

reasoned, that Jesus Himself drew near and went with them. ¹⁶But their eyes were restrained, so that they did not know Him.

¹⁷And He said to them, "What kind of conversation *is* this that you have with one another as you walk and are sad?"ᵃ

¹⁸Then the one whose name was Cleopas answered and said to Him, "Are You the only stranger in Jerusalem, and have You not known the things which happened there in these days?"

¹⁹And He said to them, "What things?"

So they said to Him, "The things concerning Jesus of Nazareth, who was a Prophet mighty in deed and word before God and all the people, ²⁰and how the chief priests and our rulers delivered Him to be condemned to death, and crucified Him. ²¹But we were hoping that it was He who was going to redeem Israel. Indeed, besides all this, today is the third day since these things happened. ²²Yes, and certain women of our company, who arrived at the tomb early, astonished us. ²³When they did not find His body, they came saying that they had also seen a vision of angels who said He was alive. ²⁴And certain of those *who were* with us went to the tomb and found *it* just as the women had said; but Him they did not see."

²⁵Then He said to them, "O foolish ones, and slow of heart to believe in all that

had come together, they asked Him, saying, "Lord, will You at this time restore the kingdom to Israel?" 7And He said to them, "It is not for you to know times or seasons which the Father has put in His own authority. 8But you shall receive power when the Holy Spirit has come upon you; and you shall be witnesses to Me^a in Jerusalem, and in all Judea and Samaria, and to the end of the earth."

JESUS ASCENDS TO HEAVEN

9Now when He had spoken these things, while they watched, He was taken up, and a cloud received Him out of their sight. 10And while they looked steadfastly toward heaven as He went up, behold, two men stood by them in white apparel, 11who also said, "Men of Galilee, why do you stand gazing up into heaven? This same Jesus, who was taken up from you into heaven, will so come in like manner as you saw Him go into heaven."

THE UPPER ROOM PRAYER MEETING

12Then they returned to Jerusalem from the mount called Olivet, which is near Jerusalem, a Sabbath day's journey. 13And when they had entered, they went up into the upper room where they were staying: Peter, James, John, and Andrew; Philip and Thomas; Bartholomew and Matthew; James the son of Alphaeus and

1:8 ^a NU-Text reads My witnesses.

Simon the Zealot; and Judas *the son* of James. [14]These all continued with one accord in prayer and supplication,[a] with the women and Mary the mother of Jesus, and with His brothers.

MATTHIAS CHOSEN

[15]And in those days Peter stood up in the midst of the disciples[a] (altogether the number of names was about a hundred and twenty), and said, [16]"Men *and* brethren, this Scripture had to be fulfilled, which the Holy Spirit spoke before by the mouth of David concerning Judas, who became a guide to those who arrested Jesus; [17]for he was numbered with us and obtained a part in this ministry."

[18](Now this man purchased a field with the wages of iniquity; and falling headlong, he burst open in the middle and all his entrails gushed out. [19]And it became known to all those dwelling in Jerusalem; so that field is called in their own language, Akel Dama, that is, Field of Blood.)

[20]"For it is written in the Book of Psalms:

'Let his dwelling place be desolate,
    And let no one live in it';[a]

and,

'Let[b] another take his office.'[c]

21"Therefore, of these men who have accompanied us all the time that the Lord Jesus went in and out among us, 22beginning from the baptism of John to that day when He was taken up from us, one of these must become a witness with us of His resurrection."

23And they proposed two: Joseph called Barsabas, who was surnamed Justus, and Matthias. 24And they prayed and said, "You, O Lord, who know the hearts of all, show which of these two You have chosen 25to take part in this ministry and apostleship from which Judas by transgression fell, that he might go to his own place." 26And they cast their lots, and the lot fell on Matthias. And he was numbered with the eleven apostles.

COMING OF THE HOLY SPIRIT

2 When the Day of Pentecost had fully come, they were all with one accord[a] in one place. 2And suddenly there came a sound from heaven, as of a rushing

1:14 [a] NU-Text omits *and supplication*. 1:15 [a] NU-Text reads *brethren.* 1:20 [a] Psalm 69:25 [b] Psalm 109:8 [c] Greek *episkopen,* position of overseer 2:1 [a] NU-Text reads *together.*

mighty wind, and it filled the whole house where they were sitting. ³Then there appeared to them divided tongues, as of fire, and *one* sat upon each of them. ⁴And they were all filled with the Holy Spirit and began to speak with other tongues, as the Spirit gave them utterance.

THE CROWD'S RESPONSE

⁵And there were dwelling in Jerusalem Jews, devout men, from every nation under heaven. ⁶And when this sound occurred, the multitude came together, and were confused, because everyone heard them speak in his own language. ⁷Then they were all amazed and marveled, saying to one another, "Look, are not all these who speak Galileans? ⁸And how *is it that* we hear, each in our own language in which we were born? ⁹Parthians and Medes and Elamites, those dwelling in Mesopotamia, Judea and Cappadocia, Pontus and Asia, ¹⁰Phrygia and Pamphylia, Egypt and the parts of Libya adjoining Cyrene, visitors from Rome, both Jews and proselytes, ¹¹Cretans and Arabs—we hear them speaking in our own tongues the wonderful works of God." ¹²So they were all amazed and perplexed, saying to one another, "Whatever could this mean?"

¹³Others mocking said, "They are full of new wine."

PETER'S SERMON

¹⁴But Peter, standing up with the eleven, raised his voice and said to them, "Men of Judea and all who dwell in Jerusalem, let this be known to you, and heed my words. ¹⁵For these are not drunk, as you suppose, since it is *only* the third hour of the day. ¹⁶But this is what was spoken by the prophet Joel:

17 'And it shall come to pass in the last days, says God,
   That I will pour out of My Spirit on all flesh;
   Your sons and your daughters shall prophesy,
   Your young men shall see visions,
   Your old men shall dream dreams.

18 And on My menservants and on My maidservants
   I will pour out My Spirit in those days;
   And they shall prophesy.

19 I will show wonders in heaven above
   And signs in the earth beneath:
   Blood and fire and vapor of smoke.

20 The sun shall be turned into darkness,
   And the moon into blood,

Before the coming of the great and
awesome day of the LORD.

21 And it shall come to pass
That whoever calls on the name of the LORD
Shall be saved.'[a]

22"Men of Israel, hear these words: Jesus of Nazareth, a Man attested by God to you by miracles, wonders, and signs which God did through Him in your midst, as you yourselves also know— 23Him, being delivered by the determined purpose and foreknowledge of God, you have taken[a] by lawless hands, have crucified, and put to death; 24whom God raised up, having loosed the pains of death, because it was not possible that He should be held by it. 25For David says concerning Him:

'I foresaw the LORD always before my face,
For He is at my right hand, that I may not be shaken.
26 Therefore my heart rejoiced, and my tongue was glad;
Moreover my flesh also will rest in hope.
27 For You will not leave my soul in Hades,
Nor will You allow Your Holy One to see corruption.

28 You have made known to me the ways of life;
You will make me full of joy in Your presence.'[a]

29"Men *and* brethren, let *me* speak freely to you of the patriarch David, that he is both dead and buried, and his tomb is with us to this day. 30Therefore, being a prophet, and knowing that God had sworn with an oath to him that of the fruit of his body, according to the flesh, He would raise up the Christ to sit on his throne,[a] 31he, foreseeing this, spoke concerning the resurrection of the Christ, that His soul was not left in Hades, nor did His flesh see corruption. 32This Jesus God has raised up, of which we are all witnesses. 33Therefore being exalted to the right hand of God, and having received from the Father the promise of the Holy Spirit, He poured out this which you now see and hear.

34"For David did not ascend into the heavens, but he says himself:

'The LORD said to my Lord,
"Sit at My right hand,
35 Till I make Your enemies Your footstool."'[a]

2:21 [a] Joel 2:28–32   2:23 [a] NU-Text omits *have taken.*   2:28 [a] Psalm 16:8–11   2:30 [a] NU-Text omits *according to the flesh, He would raise up the Christ* and completes the verse with *He would seat one on his throne.*   2:35 [a] Psalm 110:1

36"Therefore let all the house of Israel know assuredly that God has made this Jesus, whom you crucified, both Lord and Christ."

37Now when they heard *this*, they were cut to the heart, and said to Peter and the rest of the apostles, "Men *and* brethren, what shall we do?"

38Then Peter said to them, "Repent, and let every one of you be baptized in the name of Jesus Christ for the remission of sins; and you shall receive the gift of the Holy Spirit. 39For the promise is to you and to your children, and to all who are afar off, as many as the Lord our God will call."

A VITAL CHURCH GROWS

40And with many other words he testified and exhorted them, saying, "Be saved from this perverse generation." 41Then those who gladly[a] received his word were baptized; and that day about three thousand souls were added *to them*. 42And they continued steadfastly in the apostles' doctrine and fellowship, in the breaking of bread, and in prayers. 43Then fear came upon every soul, and many wonders and signs were done through the apostles. 44Now all who believed were together, and had all things in common, 45and sold their possessions and goods, and divided them among all, as anyone had need.

46So continuing daily with one accord in the temple, and breaking bread from house to house, they ate their food with gladness and simplicity of heart, [47]praising God and having favor with all the people. And the Lord added to the church[a] daily those who were being saved.

A LAME MAN HEALED

3 Now Peter and John went up together to the temple at the hour of prayer, the ninth *hour*. [2]And a certain man lame from his mother's womb was carried, whom they laid daily at the gate of the temple which is called Beautiful, to ask alms from those who entered the temple; [3]who, seeing Peter and John about to go into the temple, asked for alms. [4]And fixing his eyes on him, with John, Peter said, "Look at us." [5]So he gave them his attention, expecting to receive something from them. [6]Then Peter said, "Silver and gold I do not have, but what I do have I give you: In the name of Jesus Christ of Nazareth, rise up and walk." [7]And he took him by the right hand and lifted *him* up, and immediately his feet and ankle bones received strength. [8]So he, leaping up, stood and walked and entered the temple with them—walking, leaping, and praising God. [9]And all the people saw him walking and praising God. [10]Then they knew that it was he who sat begging alms at the Beautiful Gate of the temple; and they were filled with wonder and amazement at what had happened to him.

2:41 [a] NU-Text omits *gladly.*   2:47 [a] NU-Text omits *to the church.*

ACTS 3:11

PREACHING IN SOLOMON'S PORTICO

¹¹Now as the lame man who was healed held on to Peter and John, all the people ran together to them in the porch which is called Solomon's, greatly amazed. ¹²So when Peter saw *it*, he responded to the people: "Men of Israel, why do you marvel at this? Or why look so intently at us, as though by our own power or godliness we had made this man walk? ¹³The God of Abraham, Isaac, and Jacob, the God of our fathers, glorified His Servant Jesus, whom you delivered up and denied in the presence of Pilate, when he was determined to let *Him* go. ¹⁴But you denied the Holy One and the Just, and asked for a murderer to be granted to you, ¹⁵and killed the Prince of life, whom God raised from the dead, of which we are witnesses. ¹⁶And His name, through faith in His name, has made this man strong, whom you see and know. Yes, the faith which *comes* through Him has given him this perfect soundness in the presence of you all.

¹⁷"Yet now, brethren, I know that you did *it* in ignorance, as *did* also your rulers. ¹⁸But those things which God foretold by the mouth of all His prophets, that the Christ would suffer, He has thus fulfilled. ¹⁹Repent therefore and be converted, that your sins may be blotted out, so that times of refreshing may come from the presence of the Lord, ²⁰and that He may send Jesus Christ, who was preached to you before,ᵃ ²¹whom heaven must receive until the times of restoration of all

things, which God has spoken by the mouth of all His holy prophets since the world began. 22For Moses truly said to the fathers, 'The LORD your God will raise up for you a Prophet like me from your brethren. Him you shall hear in all things, whatever He says to you. 23And it shall be *that* every soul who will not hear that Prophet shall be utterly destroyed from among the people.'[a] 24Yes, and all the prophets, from Samuel and those who follow, as many as have spoken, have also foretold[a] these days. 25You are sons of the prophets, and of the covenant which God made with our fathers, saying to Abraham, 'And in your seed all the families of the earth shall be blessed.'[a] 26To you first, God, having raised up His Servant Jesus, sent Him to bless you, in turning away every one *of you* from your iniquities."

PETER AND JOHN ARRESTED

4 Now as they spoke to the people, the priests, the captain of the temple, and the Sadducees came upon them, 2being greatly disturbed that they taught the people and preached in Jesus the resurrection from the dead. 3And they laid hands on them, and put *them* in custody until the next day; for it was already evening. 4However, many of those who heard the word believed; and the number of the men came to be about five thousand.

3:20 a NU-Text and M-Text read *Christ Jesus, who was ordained for you before.*   3:23 a Deuteronomy 18:15, 18, 19   3:24 a NU-Text and M-Text read *proclaimed.*   3:25 a Genesis 22:18; 26:4; 28:14

ADDRESSING THE SANHEDRIN

5And it came to pass, on the next day, that their rulers, elders, and scribes, 6as well as Annas the high priest, Caiaphas, John, and Alexander, and as many as were of the family of the high priest, were gathered together at Jerusalem. 7And when they had set them in the midst, they asked, "By what power or by what name have you done this?"

8Then Peter, filled with the Holy Spirit, said to them, "Rulers of the people and elders of Israel: 9If we this day are judged for a good deed *done* to a helpless man, by what means he has been made well, 10let it be known to you all, and to all the people of Israel, that by the name of Jesus Christ of Nazareth, whom you crucified, whom God raised from the dead, by Him this man stands here before you whole. 11This is the 'stone which was rejected by you builders, which has become the chief cornerstone.' *a* 12Nor is there salvation in any other, for there is no other name under heaven given among men by which we must be saved."

THE NAME OF JESUS FORBIDDEN

13Now when they saw the boldness of Peter and John, and perceived that they were uneducated and untrained men, they marveled. And they realized that they had been with Jesus. 14And seeing the man who had been healed standing with them, they could say nothing against it. [15]But when they had commanded them to go aside out of the council, they conferred among themselves, [16]saying, "What shall we do to these men? For, indeed, that a notable miracle has been done through them *is* evident to all who dwell in Jerusalem, and we cannot deny *it*. [17]But so that it spreads no further among the people, let us severely threaten them, that from now on they speak to no man in this name."

[18]So they called them and commanded them not to speak at all nor teach in the name of Jesus. [19]But Peter and John answered and said to them, "Whether it is right in the sight of God to listen to you more than to God, you judge. [20]For we cannot but speak the things which we have seen and heard." [21]So when they had further threatened them, they let them go, finding no way of punishing them, because of the people, since they all glorified God for what had been done. [22]For the man was over forty years old on whom this miracle of healing had been performed.

PRAYER FOR BOLDNESS

[23]And being let go, they went to their own *companions* and reported all that the chief priests and elders had said to them. [24]So when they heard that, they raised their voice to God with one accord and said: "Lord, You *are* God, who

4:11 [a] Psalm 118:22

made heaven and earth and the sea, and all that is in them, 25who by the mouth of Your servant David[a] have said:

> 'Why did the nations rage,
> And the people plot vain things?
> 26 The kings of the earth took their stand,
> And the rulers were gathered together
> Against the LORD and against His Christ.'[a]

27"For truly against Your holy Servant Jesus, whom You anointed, both Herod and Pontius Pilate, with the Gentiles and the people of Israel, were gathered together 28to do whatever Your hand and Your purpose determined before to be done. 29Now, Lord, look on their threats, and grant to Your servants that with all boldness they may speak Your word, 30by stretching out Your hand to heal, and that signs and wonders may be done through the name of Your holy Servant Jesus."

31And when they had prayed, the place where they were assembled together was shaken; and they were all filled with the Holy Spirit, and they spoke the word of God with boldness.

SHARING IN ALL THINGS

32Now the multitude of those who believed were of one heart and one soul; neither did anyone say that any of the things he possessed was his own, but they had all things in common. 33And with great power the apostles gave witness to the resurrection of the Lord Jesus. And great grace was upon them all. 34Nor was there anyone among them who lacked; for all who were possessors of lands or houses sold them, and brought the proceeds of the things that were sold, 35and laid *them* at the apostles' feet; and they distributed to each as anyone had need.

36And Joses,ᵃ who was also named Barnabas by the apostles (which is translated Son of Encouragement), a Levite of the country of Cyprus, 37having land, sold *it*, and brought the money and laid *it* at the apostles' feet.

LYING TO THE HOLY SPIRIT

5 But a certain man named Ananias, with Sapphira his wife, sold a possession. 2And he kept back *part* of the proceeds, his wife also being aware *of it*, and brought a certain part and laid *it* at the apostles' feet. 3But Peter said, "Ananias, why has Satan filled your heart to lie to the Holy Spirit and keep back *part* of

4:25 ᵃ NU-Text reads *who through the Holy Spirit, by the mouth of our father, Your servant David.*
4:26 ᵃ Psalm 2:1, 2   4:36 ᵃ NU-Text reads *Joseph.*

the price of the land for yourself? ⁴while it remained, was it not your own? And after it was sold, was it not in your own control? Why have you conceived this thing in your heart? You have not lied to men but to God."

⁵Then Ananias, hearing these words, fell down and breathed his last. So great fear came upon all those who heard these things. ⁶And the young men arose and wrapped *him* out, and buried *him*.

⁷Now it was about three hours later when his wife came in, not knowing what had happened. ⁸And Peter answered her, "Tell me whether you sold the land for so much?"

She said, "Yes, for so much."

⁹Then Peter said to her, "How is it that you have agreed together to test the Spirit of the Lord? Look, the feet of those who have buried your husband *are* at the door, and they will carry you out." ¹⁰Then immediately she fell down at his feet and breathed her last. And the young men came in and found her dead, and carrying *her* out, buried *her* by her husband. ¹¹So great fear came upon all the church and upon all who heard these things.

CONTINUING POWER IN THE CHURCH

¹²And through the hands of the apostles many signs and wonders were done

among the people. And they were all with one accord in Solomon's Porch. ¹³Yet none of the rest dared join them, but the people esteemed them highly. ¹⁴And believers were increasingly added to the Lord, multitudes of both men and women, ¹⁵so that they brought the sick out into the streets and laid *them* on beds and couches, that at least the shadow of Peter passing by might fall on some of them. ¹⁶Also a multitude gathered from the surrounding cities to Jerusalem, bringing sick people and those who were tormented by unclean spirits, and they were all healed.

IMPRISONED APOSTLES FREED

¹⁷Then the high priest rose up, and all those who *were* with him (which is the sect of the Sadducees), and they were filled with indignation, ¹⁸and laid their hands on the apostles and put them in the common prison. ¹⁹But at night an angel of the Lord opened the prison doors and brought them out, and said, ²⁰"Go, stand in the temple and speak to the people all the words of this life."

²¹And when they heard *that,* they entered the temple early in the morning and taught. But the high priest and those with him came and called the council together, with all the elders of the children of Israel, and sent to the prison to have them brought.

APOSTLES ON TRIAL AGAIN

22But when the officers came and did not find them in the prison, they returned and reported, 23saying, "Indeed we found the prison shut securely, and the guards standing outside*a* before the doors; but when we opened them, we found no one inside!" 24Now when the high priest,*a* the captain of the temple, and the chief priests heard these things, they wondered what the outcome would be. 25So one came and told them, saying,*a* "Look, the men whom you put in prison are standing in the temple and teaching the people!"

26Then the captain went with the officers and brought them without violence, for they feared the people, lest they should be stoned. 27And when they had brought them, they set *them* before the council. And the high priest asked them, 28saying, "Did we not strictly command you not to teach in this name? And look, you have filled Jerusalem with your doctrine, and intend to bring this Man's blood on us!"

29But Peter and the *other* apostles answered and said: "We ought to obey God rather than men. 30The God of our fathers raised up Jesus whom you murdered by hanging on a tree. 31Him God has exalted to His right hand *to be* Prince and Savior, to give repentance to Israel and forgiveness of sins. 32And we are His witnesses to these things, and so also is the Holy Spirit whom God has given to those who obey Him."

GAMALIEL'S ADVICE

33 When they heard this, they were furious and plotted to kill them. 34 Then one in the council stood up, a Pharisee named Gamaliel, a teacher of the law held in respect by all the people, and commanded them to put the apostles outside for a little while. 35 And he said to them: "Men of Israel, take heed to yourselves what you intend to do regarding these men. 36 For some time ago Theudas rose up, claiming to be somebody. A number of men, about four hundred, joined him. He was slain, and all who obeyed him were scattered and came to nothing. 37 After this man, Judas of Galilee rose up in the days of the census, and drew away many people after him. He also perished, and all who obeyed him were dispersed. 38 And now I say to you, keep away from these men and let them alone; for if this plan or this work is of men, it will come to nothing; 39 but if it is of God, you cannot overthrow it—lest you even be found to fight against God."

40 And they agreed with him, and when they had called for the apostles and beaten them, they commanded that they should not speak in the name of Jesus,

5:23 a NU-Text and M-Text omit outside.   5:24 a NU-Text omits the high priest.   5:25 a NU-Text and M-Text omit saying.

and let them go. 41So they departed from the presence of the council, rejoicing that they were counted worthy to suffer shame for His[a] name. 42And daily in the temple, and in every house, they did not cease teaching and preaching Jesus as the Christ.

SEVEN CHOSEN TO SERVE

6 Now in those days, when the number of the disciples was multiplying, there arose a complaint against the Hebrews by the Hellenists,[a] because their widows were neglected in the daily distribution. 2Then the twelve summoned the multitude of the disciples and said, "It is not desirable that we should leave the word of God and serve tables. 3Therefore, brethren, seek out from among you seven men of good reputation, full of the Holy Spirit and wisdom, whom we may appoint over this business; 4but we will give ourselves continually to prayer and to the ministry of the word."

5And the saying pleased the whole multitude. And they chose Stephen, a man full of faith and the Holy Spirit and Philip, Prochorus, Nicanor, Timon, Parmenas, and Nicolas, a proselyte from Antioch, 6whom they set before the apostles; and when they had prayed, they laid hands on them.

7Then the word of God spread, and the number of the disciples multiplied greatly in Jerusalem, and a great many of the priests were obedient to the faith.

STEPHEN ACCUSED OF BLASPHEMY

8And Stephen, full of faith^a and power, did great wonders and signs among the people. 9Then there arose some from what is called the Synagogue of the Freedmen (Cyrenians, Alexandrians, and those from Cilicia and Asia), disputing with Stephen. 10And they were not able to resist the wisdom and the Spirit by which he spoke. 11Then they secretly induced men to say, "We have heard him speak blasphemous words against Moses and God." 12And they stirred up the people, and the elders, and the scribes; and they came upon *him*, seized him, and brought *him* to the council. 13They also set up false witnesses who said, "This man does not cease to speak blasphemous^a words against this holy place and the law; 14for we have heard him say that this Jesus of Nazareth will destroy this place and change the customs which Moses delivered to us." 15And all who sat in the council, looking steadfastly at him, saw his face as the face of an angel.

5:41 ^a NU-Text reads *the name*; M-Text reads *the name of Jesus.*   6:1 ^a *That is, Greek-speaking Jews*
6:8 ^a NU-Text reads *grace.*   6:13 ^a NU-Text omits *blasphemous.*

STEPHEN'S ADDRESS: THE CALL OF ABRAHAM

7 Then the high priest said, "Are these things so?"

2 And he said, "Brethren and fathers, listen: The God of glory appeared to our father Abraham when he was in Mesopotamia, before he dwelt in Haran, 3 and said to him, 'Get out of your country and from your relatives, and come to a land that I will show you.' *a* 4 Then he came out of the land of the Chaldeans and dwelt in Haran. And from there, when his father was dead, He moved him to this land in which you now dwell. 5 And *God* gave him no inheritance in it, not even *enough* to set his foot on. But even when *Abraham* had no child, He promised to give it to him for a possession, and to his descendants after him. 6 But God spoke in this way: that his descendants would dwell in a foreign land, and that they would bring them into bondage and oppress *them* four hundred years. 7 'And the nation to whom they will be in bondage I will judge,' *a* said God, 'and after that they shall come out and serve Me in this place.' *b* 8 Then He gave him the covenant of circumcision; and so *Abraham* begot Isaac and circumcised him on the eighth day; and Isaac *begot* Jacob, and Jacob *begot* the twelve patriarchs.

THE PATRIARCHS IN EGYPT

9 "And the patriarchs, becoming envious, sold Joseph into Egypt. But God was

with him [10]and delivered him out of all his troubles, and gave him favor and wisdom in the presence of Pharaoh, king of Egypt; and he made him governor over Egypt and all his house. [11]Now a famine and great trouble came over all the land of Egypt and Canaan, and our fathers found no sustenance. [12]But when Jacob heard that there was grain in Egypt, he sent out our fathers first. [13]And the second *time* Joseph was made known to his brothers, and Joseph's family became known to the Pharaoh. [14]Then Joseph sent and called his father Jacob and all his relatives to *him*, seventy-five[a] people. [15]So Jacob went down to Egypt; and he died, he and our fathers. [16]And they were carried back to Shechem and laid in the tomb that Abraham bought for a sum of money from the sons of Hamor, *the father* of Shechem.

GOD DELIVERS ISRAEL BY MOSES

[17]"But when the time of the promise drew near which God had sworn to Abraham, the people grew and multiplied in Egypt [18]till another king arose who did not know Joseph. [19]This man dealt treacherously with our people, and oppressed our forefathers, making them expose their babies, so that they might not live. [20]At this time Moses was born, and was well pleasing to God; and he was brought up in his father's house for three months. [21]But when he was set

7:3 [a] Genesis 12:1   7:7 [a] Genesis 15:14   [b] Exodus 3:12   7:14 [a] Or *seventy* (compare Exodus 1:5)

out, Pharaoh's daughter took him away and brought him up as her own son. [22]And Moses was learned in all the wisdom of the Egyptians, and was mighty in words and deeds.

[23]"Now when he was forty years old, it came into his heart to visit his brethren, the children of Israel. [24]And seeing one of *them* suffer wrong, he defended and avenged him who was oppressed, and struck down the Egyptian. [25]For he supposed that his brethren would have understood that God would deliver them by his hand, but they did not understand. [26]And the next day he appeared to *two of* them as they were fighting, and *tried to* reconcile them, saying, 'Men, you are brethren; why do you wrong one another?' [27]But he who did his neighbor wrong pushed him away, saying, 'Who made you a ruler and a judge over us? [28]Do you want to kill me as you did the Egyptian yesterday?'[a] [29]Then, at this saying, Moses fled and became a dweller in the land of Midian, where he had two sons.

[30]"And when forty years had passed, an Angel of the Lord[a] appeared to him in a flame of fire in a bush, in the wilderness of Mount Sinai. [31]When Moses saw *it,* he marveled at the sight; and as he drew near to observe, the voice of the Lord came to him, [32]*saying,* 'I *am* the God of your fathers—the God of Abraham, the God of Isaac, and the God of Jacob.'[a] And Moses trembled and dared not

look. [33]"Then the LORD said to him, "Take your sandals off your feet, for the place where you stand is holy ground. [34]I have surely seen the oppression of My people who are in Egypt; I have heard their groaning and have come down to deliver them. And now come, I will send you to Egypt."[a]

[35]"This Moses whom they rejected, saying, 'Who made you a ruler and a judge?'[a] is the one God sent *to be* a ruler and a deliverer by the hand of the Angel who appeared to him in the bush. [36]He brought them out, after he had shown wonders and signs in the land of Egypt, and in the Red Sea, and in the wilderness forty years.

ISRAEL REBELS AGAINST GOD

[37]"This is that Moses who said to the children of Israel,[a] 'The LORD your God will raise up for you a Prophet like me from your brethren. Him you shall hear.'[b]

[38]"This is he who was in the congregation in the wilderness with the Angel who spoke to him on Mount Sinai, and *with* our fathers, the one who received the living oracles to give to us, [39]whom our fathers would not obey, but rejected. And in their hearts they turned back to Egypt, [40]saying to Aaron, 'Make us gods to go before us; *as for* this Moses who brought us out of the land of Egypt, we

7:28 [a] Exodus 2:14   7:30 [a] NU-Text omits *of the Lord.*   7:32 [a] Exodus 3:6, 15   7:34 [a] Exodus 3:5, 7, 8, 10
7:35 [a] Exodus 2:14   7:37 [a] Deuteronomy 18:15   [b] NU-Text and M-Text omit *Him you shall hear.*

do not know what has become of him.'*a* 41And they made a calf in those days, offered sacrifices to the idol, and rejoiced in the works of their own hands. 42Then God turned and gave them up to worship the host of heaven, as it is written in the book of the Prophets:

'Did you offer Me slaughtered animals and sacrifices
during forty years in the wilderness,
O house of Israel?
43 You also took up the tabernacle of Moloch,
And the star of your god Remphan,
Images which you made to worship;
And I will carry you away beyond Babylon.'*a*

GOD'S TRUE TABERNACLE

44"Our fathers had the tabernacle of witness in the wilderness, as He appointed, instructing Moses to make it according to the pattern that he had seen, 45which our fathers, having received it in turn, also brought with Joshua into the land possessed by the Gentiles, whom God drove out before the face of our fathers until the days of David, 46who found favor before God and asked to find a dwelling for the God of Jacob. [47]But Solomon built Him a house. [48]"However, the Most High does not dwell in temples made with hands, as the prophet says:

[49] 'Heaven *is* My throne,
And earth *is* My footstool.
What house will you build for Me? says the LORD,
Or what *is* the place of My rest?
[50] Has My hand not made all these things?'[a]

ISRAEL RESISTS THE HOLY SPIRIT

[51]"You stiff-necked and uncircumcised in heart and ears! You always resist the Holy Spirit; as your fathers *did*, so *do* you. [52]Which of the prophets did your fathers not persecute? And they killed those who foretold the coming of the Just One, of whom you now have become the betrayers and murderers, [53]who have received the law by the direction of angels and have not kept *it*."

STEPHEN THE MARTYR

[54]When they heard these things they were cut to the heart, and they gnashed

7:40 [a] Exodus 32:1, 23   7:43 [a] Amos 5:25–27   7:50 [a] Isaiah 66:1, 2

at him with *their* teeth. 55But he, being full of the Holy Spirit, gazed into heaven and saw the glory of God, and Jesus standing at the right hand of God, 56and said, "Look! I see the heavens opened and the Son of Man standing at the right hand of God!"

57Then they cried out with a loud voice, stopped their ears, and ran at him with one accord; 58and they cast *him* out of the city and stoned *him.* And the witnesses laid down their clothes at the feet of a young man named Saul. 59And they stoned Stephen as he was calling on *God* and saying, "Lord Jesus, receive my spirit." 60Then he knelt down and cried out with a loud voice, "Lord, do not charge them with this sin." And when he had said this, he fell asleep.

SAUL PERSECUTES THE CHURCH

8 Now Saul was consenting to his death.

At that time a great persecution arose against the church which was at Jerusalem; and they were all scattered throughout the regions of Judea and Samaria, except the apostles. 2And devout men carried Stephen *to his burial,* and made great lamentation over him.

3As for Saul, he made havoc of the church, entering every house, and dragging off men and women, committing *them* to prison.

CHRIST IS PREACHED IN SAMARIA

⁴Therefore those who were scattered went everywhere preaching the word. ⁵Then Philip went down to the[a] city of Samaria and preached Christ to them. ⁶And the multitudes with one accord heeded the things spoken by Philip, hearing and seeing the miracles which he did. ⁷For unclean spirits, crying with a loud voice, came out of many who were possessed; and many who were paralyzed and lame were healed. ⁸And there was great joy in that city.

THE SORCERER'S PROFESSION OF FAITH

⁹But there was a certain man called Simon, who previously practiced sorcery in the city and astonished the people of Samaria, claiming that he was someone great, ¹⁰to whom they all gave heed, from the least to the greatest, saying, "This man is the great power of God." ¹¹And they heeded him because he had astonished them with his sorceries for a long time. ¹²But when they believed Philip as he preached the things concerning the kingdom of God and the name of Jesus Christ, both men and women were baptized. ¹³Then Simon himself also believed; and when he was baptized he continued with Philip, and was amazed, seeing the miracles and signs which were done.

8:5 ª Or *a*

THE SORCERER'S SIN

¹⁴Now when the apostles who were at Jerusalem heard that Samaria had received the word of God, they sent Peter and John to them, ¹⁵who, when they had come down, prayed for them that they might receive the Holy Spirit. ¹⁶For as yet He had fallen upon none of them. They had only been baptized in the name of the Lord Jesus. ¹⁷Then they laid hands on them, and they received the Holy Spirit.

¹⁸And when Simon saw that through the laying on of the apostles' hands the Holy Spirit was given, he offered them money, ¹⁹saying, "Give me this power also, that anyone on whom I lay hands may receive the Holy Spirit."

²⁰But Peter said to him, "Your money perish with you, because you thought that the gift of God could be purchased with money! ²¹You have neither part nor portion in this matter, for your heart is not right in the sight of God. ²²Repent therefore of this your wickedness, and pray God if perhaps the thought of your heart may be forgiven you. ²³For I see that you are poisoned by bitterness and bound by iniquity."

²⁴Then Simon answered and said, "Pray to the Lord for me, that none of the things which you have spoken may come upon me."

²⁵So when they had testified and preached the word of the Lord, they returned to Jerusalem, preaching the gospel in many villages of the Samaritans.

CHRIST IS PREACHED TO AN ETHIOPIAN

26Now an angel of the Lord spoke to Philip, saying, "Arise and go toward the south along the road which goes down from Jerusalem to Gaza." This is desert. 27So he arose and went. And behold, a man of Ethiopia, a eunuch of great authority under Candace the queen of the Ethiopians, who had charge of all her treasury, and had come to Jerusalem to worship, 28was returning. And sitting in his chariot, he was reading Isaiah the prophet. 29Then the Spirit said to Philip, "Go near and overtake this chariot."

30So Philip ran to him, and heard him reading the prophet Isaiah, and said, "Do you understand what you are reading?"

31And he said, "How can I, unless someone guides me?" And he asked Philip to come up and sit with him. 32The place in the Scripture which he read was this:

"He was led as a sheep to the slaughter;
And as a lamb before its shearer is silent,
So He opened not His mouth.
33 In His humiliation His justice was taken away,
And who will declare His generation?
For His life is taken from the earth."[a]

8:33 [a] Isaiah 53:7, 8

³⁴So the eunuch answered Philip and said, "I ask you, of whom does the prophet say this, of himself or of some other man?" ³⁵Then Philip opened his mouth, and beginning at this Scripture, preached Jesus to him. ³⁶Now as they went down the road, they came to some water. And the eunuch said, "See, *here is* water. What hinders me from being baptized?"

³⁷Then Philip said, "If you believe with all your heart, you may."

And he answered and said, "I believe that Jesus Christ is the Son of God."ᵃ

³⁸So he commanded the chariot to stand still. And both Philip and the eunuch went down into the water, and he baptized him. ³⁹Now when they came up out of the water, the Spirit of the Lord caught Philip away, so that the eunuch saw him no more; and he went on his way rejoicing. ⁴⁰But Philip was found at Azotus. And passing through, he preached in all the cities till he came to Caesarea.

THE DAMASCUS ROAD: SAUL CONVERTED

9 Then Saul, still breathing threats and murder against the disciples of the Lord, went to the high priest ²and asked letters from him to the synagogues of Damascus, so that if he found any who were of the Way, whether men or women, he might bring them bound to Jerusalem.

3As he journeyed he came near Damascus, and suddenly a light shone around him from heaven. 4Then he fell to the ground, and heard a voice saying to him, "Saul, Saul, why are you persecuting Me?"

5And he said, "Who are You, Lord?"

Then the Lord said, "I am Jesus, whom you are persecuting.[a] It *is* hard for you to kick against the goads."

6So he, trembling and astonished, said, "Lord, what do You want me to do?"

Then the Lord *said* to him, "Arise and go into the city, and you will be told what you must do."

7And the men who journeyed with him stood speechless, hearing a voice but seeing no one. 8Then Saul arose from the ground, and when his eyes were opened he saw no one. But they led him by the hand and brought *him* into Damascus. 9And he was three days without sight, and neither ate nor drank.

ANANIAS BAPTIZES SAUL

10Now there was a certain disciple at Damascus named Ananias; and to him the Lord said in a vision, "Ananias."

And he said, "Here I am, Lord."

8:37 [a] NU-Text and M-Text omit this verse. It is found in Western texts, including the Latin tradition.
9:5 [a] NU-Text and M-Text omit the last sentence of verse 5 and begin verse 6 with *But arise and go.*

¹¹So the Lord *said* to him, "Arise and go to the street called Straight, and inquire at the house of Judas for *one* called Saul of Tarsus, for behold, he is praying, ¹²And in a vision he has seen a man named Ananias coming in and putting *his* hand on him, so that he might receive his sight."

¹³Then Ananias answered, "Lord, I have heard from many about this man, how much harm he has done to Your saints in Jerusalem. ¹⁴And here he has authority from the chief priests to bind all who call on Your name."

¹⁵But the Lord said to him, "Go, for he is a chosen vessel of Mine to bear My name before Gentiles, kings, and the children of Israel. ¹⁶For I will show him how many things he must suffer for My name's sake."

¹⁷And Ananias went his way and entered the house; and laying his hands on him he said, "Brother Saul, the Lord Jesus,^a who appeared to you on the road as you came, has sent me that you may receive your sight and be filled with the Holy Spirit." ¹⁸Immediately there fell from his eyes *something* like scales, and he received his sight at once; and he arose and was baptized.

¹⁹So when he had received food, he was strengthened. Then Saul spent some days with the disciples at Damascus.

SAUL PREACHES CHRIST

20Immediately he preached the Christ[a] in the synagogues, that He is the Son of God.

21Then all who heard were amazed, and said, "Is this not he who destroyed those who called on this name in Jerusalem, and has come here for that purpose, so that he might bring them bound to the chief priests?"

22But Saul increased all the more in strength, and confounded the Jews who dwelt in Damascus, proving that this *Jesus* is the Christ.

SAUL ESCAPES DEATH

23Now after many days were past, the Jews plotted to kill him. 24But their plot became known to Saul. And they watched the gates day and night, to kill him. 25Then the disciples took him by night and let *him* down through the wall in a large basket.

SAUL AT JERUSALEM

26And when Saul had come to Jerusalem, he tried to join the disciples; but they were all afraid of him, and did not believe that he was a disciple. 27But Barnabas took him and brought *him* to the apostles. And he declared to them

9:17 *a* M-Text omits *Jesus.*   9:20 *a* NU-Text reads *Jesus.*

how he had seen the Lord on the road, and how he had spoken to him, and that He had spoken to him in the name of Jesus. 28So he was with them at Jerusalem, coming in and going out. 29And he spoke boldly in the name of the Lord Jesus and disputed against the Hellenists, but they attempted to kill him. 30When the brethren found out, they brought him down to Caesarea and sent him out to Tarsus.

THE CHURCH PROSPERS

31Then the churches[a] throughout all Judea, Galilee, and Samaria had peace and were edified. And walking in the fear of the Lord and in the comfort of the Holy Spirit, they were multiplied.

AENEAS HEALED

32Now it came to pass, as Peter went through all *parts of the country,* that he also came down to the saints who dwelt in Lydda. 33There he found a certain man named Aeneas, who had been bedridden eight years and was paralyzed. 34And Peter said to him, "Aeneas, Jesus the Christ heals you. Arise and make your bed." Then he arose immediately. 35So all who dwelt at Lydda and Sharon saw him and turned to the Lord.

DORCAS RESTORED TO LIFE

36At Joppa there was a certain disciple named Tabitha, which is translated Dorcas. This woman was full of good works and charitable deeds which she did. 37But it happened in those days that she became sick and died. When they had washed her, they laid *her* in an upper room. 38And since Lydda was near Joppa, and the disciples had heard that Peter was there, they sent two men to him, imploring *him* not to delay in coming to them. 39Then Peter arose and went with them. When he had come, they brought *him* to the upper room. And all the widows stood by him weeping, showing the tunics and garments which Dorcas had made while she was with them. 40But Peter put them all out, and knelt down and prayed. And turning to the body he said, "Tabitha, arise." And she opened her eyes, and when she saw Peter she sat up. 41Then he gave her *his* hand and lifted her up; and when he had called the saints and widows, he presented her alive. 42And it became known throughout all Joppa, and many believed on the Lord. 43So it was that he stayed many days in Joppa with Simon, a tanner.

CORNELIUS SENDS A DELEGATION

10 There was a certain man in Caesarea called Cornelius, a centurion of what was called the Italian Regiment, 2a devout *man* and one who feared God

9:31 *a* NU-Text reads *church. . . . was edified.*

with all his household, who gave alms generously to the people, and prayed to God always. ³About the ninth hour of the day he saw clearly in a vision an angel of God coming in and saying to him, "Cornelius!"

⁴And when he observed him, he was afraid, and said, "What is it, lord?"

So he said to him, "Your prayers and your alms have come up for a memorial before God. ⁵Now send men to Joppa, and send for Simon whose surname is Peter. ⁶He is lodging with Simon, a tanner, whose house is by the sea.ᵃ He will tell you what you must do." ⁷And when the angel who spoke to him had departed, Cornelius called two of his household servants and a devout soldier from among those who waited on him continually. ⁸So when he had explained all *these* things to them, he sent them to Joppa.

PETER'S VISION

⁹The next day, as they went on their journey and drew near the city, Peter went up on the housetop to pray, about the sixth hour. ¹⁰Then he became very hungry and wanted to eat; but while they made ready, he fell into a trance ¹¹and saw heaven opened and an object like a great sheet bound at the four corners, descending to him and let down to the earth. ¹²In it were all kinds of four-footed animals of the earth, wild beasts, creeping things, and birds of

the air. ¹³And a voice came to him, "Rise, Peter; kill and eat."

¹⁴But Peter said, "Not so, Lord! For I have never eaten anything common or unclean."

¹⁵And a voice *spoke* to him again the second time, "What God has cleansed you must not call common." ¹⁶This was done three times. And the object was taken up into heaven again.

SUMMONED TO CAESAREA

¹⁷Now while Peter wondered within himself what this vision which he had seen meant, behold, the men who had been sent from Cornelius had made inquiry for Simon's house, and stood before the gate. ¹⁸And they called and asked whether Simon, whose surname was Peter, was lodging there.

¹⁹While Peter thought about the vision, the Spirit said to him, "Behold, three men are seeking you. ²⁰Arise therefore, go down and go with them, doubting nothing; for I have sent them."

²¹Then Peter went down to the men who had been sent to him from Cornelius,ᵃ and said, "Yes, I am he whom you seek. For what reason have you come?" ²²And they said, "Cornelius *the* centurion, a just man, one who fears God

10:6 ᵃ NU-Text and M-Text omit the last sentence of this verse.   10:21 ᵃ NU-Text and M-Text omit *who had been sent to him from Cornelius.*

and has a good reputation among all the nation of the Jews, was divinely instructed by a holy angel to summon you to his house, and to hear words from you." 23Then he invited them in and lodged *them.*

On the next day Peter went away with them, and some brethren from Joppa accompanied him.

PETER MEETS CORNELIUS

24And the following day they entered Caesarea. Now Cornelius was waiting for them, and had called together his relatives and close friends. 25As Peter was coming in, Cornelius met him and fell down at his feet and worshiped *him.* 26But Peter lifted him up, saying, "Stand up; I myself am also a man." 27And as he talked with him, he went in and found many who had come together. 28Then he said to them, "You know how unlawful it is for a Jewish man to keep company with or go to one of another nation. But God has shown me that I should not call any man common or unclean. 29Therefore I came without objection as soon as I was sent for. I ask, then, for what reason have you sent for me?"

30So Cornelius said, "Four days ago I was fasting until this hour; and at the ninth hour[a] I prayed in my house, and behold, a man stood before me in bright clothing, 31and said, 'Cornelius, your prayer has been heard, and your alms are remembered in the sight of God. [32]Send therefore to Joppa and call Simon here, whose surname is Peter. He is lodging in the house of Simon, a tanner, by the sea.[a] When he comes, he will speak to you.' [33]So I sent to you immediately, and you have done well to come. Now therefore, we are all present before God, to hear all the things commanded you by God."

PREACHING TO CORNELIUS' HOUSEHOLD

[34]Then Peter opened his mouth and said: "In truth I perceive that God shows no partiality. [35]But in every nation whoever fears Him and works righteousness is accepted by Him. [36]The word which God sent to the children of Israel, preaching peace through Jesus Christ—He is Lord of all— [37]that word you know, which was proclaimed throughout all Judea, and began from Galilee after the baptism which John preached: [38]how God anointed Jesus of Nazareth with the Holy Spirit and with power, who went about doing good and healing all who were oppressed by the devil, for God was with Him. [39]And we are witnesses of all things which He did both in the land of the Jews and in Jerusalem, whom they[a] killed by hanging on a tree. [40]Him God raised up on the third day, and showed Him openly, [41]not to all the people, but to witnesses chosen before by God, even to us who

10:30 [a] NU-Text reads Four days ago to this hour, at the ninth hour.   10:32 [a] NU-Text omits the last sentence of this verse.   10:39 [a] NU-Text and M-Text add also.

ate and drank with Him after He arose from the dead. ⁴²And He commanded us to preach to the people, and to testify that it is He who was ordained by God *to be* Judge of the living and the dead. ⁴³To Him all the prophets witness that, through His name, whoever believes in Him will receive remission of sins."

THE HOLY SPIRIT FALLS ON THE GENTILES

⁴⁴While Peter was still speaking these words, the Holy Spirit fell upon all those who heard the word. ⁴⁵And those of the circumcision who believed were astonished, as many as came with Peter, because the gift of the Holy Spirit had been poured out on the Gentiles also. ⁴⁶For they heard them speak with tongues and magnify God.

Then Peter answered, ⁴⁷"Can anyone forbid water, that these should not be baptized who have received the Holy Spirit just as we *have*?" ⁴⁸And he commanded them to be baptized in the name of the Lord. Then they asked him to stay a few days.

PETER DEFENDS GOD'S GRACE

11 Now the apostles and brethren who were in Judea heard that the Gentiles had also received the word of God. ²And when Peter came up to Jerusalem, those of the circumcision contended with him, 3saying, "You went in to uncircumcised men and ate with them!"

4"But Peter explained *it* to them in order from the beginning, saying; 5"I was in the city of Joppa praying; and in a trance I saw a vision, an object descending like a great sheet, let down from heaven by four corners; and it came to me. 6When I observed it intently and considered, I saw four-footed animals of the earth, wild beasts, creeping things, and birds of the air. 7And I heard a voice saying to me, 'Rise, Peter; kill and eat.' 8But I said, 'Not so, Lord! For nothing common or unclean has at any time entered my mouth.' 9But the voice answered me again from heaven, 'What God has cleansed you must not call common.' 10Now this was done three times, and all were drawn up again into heaven. 11At that very moment, three men stood before the house where I was, having been sent to me from Caesarea. 12Then the Spirit told me to go with them, doubting nothing. Moreover these six brethren accompanied me, and we entered the man's house. 13And he told us how he had seen an angel standing in his house, who said to him, 'Send men to Joppa, and call for Simon whose surname is Peter, 14who will tell you words by which you and all your household will be saved.' 15And as I began to speak, the Holy Spirit fell upon them, as upon us at the beginning. 16Then I remembered the word of the Lord, how He said, 'John indeed baptized with water, but you shall be baptized with the Holy Spirit.' 17If therefore God gave them the same gift as *He gave* us when we believed on the Lord Jesus Christ, who was I that I could withstand God?"

18When they heard these things they became silent; and they glorified God, saying, "Then God has also granted to the Gentiles repentance to life."

BARNABAS AND SAUL AT ANTIOCH

19Now those who were scattered after the persecution that arose over Stephen traveled as far as Phoenicia, Cyprus, and Antioch, preaching the word to no one but the Jews only. 20But some of them were men from Cyprus and Cyrene, who, when they had come to Antioch, spoke to the Hellenists, preaching the Lord Jesus. 21And the hand of the Lord was with them, and a great number believed and turned to the Lord.

22Then news of these things came to the ears of the church in Jerusalem, and they sent out Barnabas to go as far as Antioch. 23When he came and had seen the grace of God, he was glad, and encouraged them all that with purpose of heart they should continue with the Lord. 24For he was a good man, full of the Holy Spirit and of faith. And a great many people were added to the Lord. 25Then Barnabas departed for Tarsus to seek Saul. 26And when he had found him, he brought him to Antioch. So it was that for a whole year they assembled with the church and taught a great many people. And the disciples were first called Christians in Antioch.

RELIEF TO JUDEA

27 And in these days prophets came from Jerusalem to Antioch. 28 Then one of them, named Agabus, stood up and showed by the Spirit that there was going to be a great famine throughout all the world, which also happened in the days of Claudius Caesar. 29 Then the disciples, each according to his ability, determined to send relief to the brethren dwelling in Judea. 30 This they also did, and sent it to the elders by the hands of Barnabas and Saul.

HEROD'S VIOLENCE TO THE CHURCH

12 Now about that time Herod the king stretched out *his* hand to harass some from the church. 2 Then he killed James the brother of John with the sword. 3 And because he saw that it pleased the Jews, he proceeded further to seize Peter also. Now it was *during* the Days of Unleavened Bread. 4 So when he had arrested him, he put *him* in prison, and delivered *him* to four squads of soldiers to keep him, intending to bring him before the people after Passover.

PETER FREED FROM PRISON

5Peter was therefore kept in prison, but constant[a] prayer was offered to God for him by the church. 6And when Herod was about to bring him out, that night Peter was sleeping, bound with two chains between two soldiers; and the guards before the door were keeping the prison. 7Now behold, an angel of the Lord stood by *him*, and a light shone in the prison; and he struck Peter on the side and raised him up, saying, "Arise quickly!" And his chains fell off *his* hands. 8Then the angel said to him, "Gird yourself and tie on your sandals"; and so he did. And he said to him, "Put on your garment and follow me." 9So he went out and followed him, and did not know that what was done by the angel was real, but thought he was seeing a vision. 10When they were past the first and the second guard posts, they came to the iron gate that leads to the city, which opened to them of its own accord; and they went out and went down one street, and immediately the angel departed from him.

11And when Peter had come to himself, he said, "Now I know for certain that the Lord has sent His angel, and has delivered me from the hand of Herod and *from* all the expectation of the Jewish people."

12So, when he had considered *this,* he came to the house of Mary, the mother of John whose surname was Mark, where many were gathered together praying.

¹³And as Peter knocked at the door of the gate, a girl named Rhoda came to answer. ¹⁴When she recognized Peter's voice, because of *her* gladness she did not open the gate, but ran in and announced that Peter stood before the gate. ¹⁵But they said to her, "You are beside yourself!" Yet she kept insisting that it was so. So they said, "It is his angel."

¹⁶Now Peter continued knocking; and when they opened *the door* and saw him, they were astonished. ¹⁷But motioning to them with his hand to keep silent, he declared to them how the Lord had brought him out of the prison. And he said, "Go, tell these things to James and to the brethren." And he departed and went to another place.

¹⁸Then, as soon as it was day, there *was* no small stir among the soldiers about what had become of Peter. ¹⁹But when Herod had searched for him and not found him, he examined the guards and commanded that *they* should be put to death.

And he went down from Judea to Caesarea, and stayed *there*.

HEROD'S VIOLENT DEATH

²⁰Now Herod had been very angry with the people of Tyre and Sidon; but they came to him with one accord, and having made Blastus the king's personal

12:5 ª NU-Text reads *constantly* (or *earnestly*).

aide their friend, they asked for peace, because their country was supplied with food by the king's *country*.

21So on a set day Herod, arrayed in royal apparel, sat on his throne and gave an oration to them. 22And the people kept shouting, "The voice of a god and not of a man!" 23Then immediately an angel of the Lord struck him, because he did not give glory to God. And he was eaten by worms and died.

24But the word of God grew and multiplied.

BARNABAS AND SAUL APPOINTED

25And Barnabas and Saul returned from[a] Jerusalem when they had fulfilled *their* ministry, and they also took with them John whose surname was Mark.

13 Now in the church that was at Antioch there were certain prophets and teachers: Barnabas, Simeon who was called Niger, Lucius of Cyrene, Manaen who had been brought up with Herod the tetrarch, and Saul. 2As they ministered to the Lord and fasted, the Holy Spirit said, "Now separate to Me Barnabas and Saul for the work to which I have called them." 3Then, having fasted and prayed, and laid hands on them, they sent *them* away.

PREACHING IN CYPRUS

4 So, being sent out by the Holy Spirit, they went down to Seleucia, and from there they sailed to Cyprus. 5 And when they arrived in Salamis, they preached the word of God in the synagogues of the Jews. They also had John as *their* assistant.

6 Now when they had gone through the island[a] to Paphos, they found a certain sorcerer, a false prophet, a Jew whose name *was* Bar-Jesus, 7 who was with the proconsul, Sergius Paulus, an intelligent man. This man called for Barnabas and Saul and sought to hear the word of God. 8 But Elymas the sorcerer (for so his name is translated) withstood them, seeking to turn the proconsul away from the faith. 9 Then Saul, who also *is called* Paul, filled with the Holy Spirit, looked intently at him 10 and said, "O full of all deceit and all fraud, *you* son of the devil, *you* enemy of all righteousness, will you not cease perverting the straight ways of the Lord? 11 And now, indeed, the hand of the Lord *is* upon you, and you shall be blind, not seeing the sun for a time."

And immediately a dark mist fell on him, and he went around seeking someone to lead him by the hand. 12 Then the proconsul believed, when he saw what had been done, being astonished at the teaching of the Lord.

12:25 a NU-Text and M-Text read *to*.   13:6 a NU-Text reads *the whole island.*

AT ANTIOCH IN PISIDIA

13Now when Paul and his party set sail from Paphos, they came to Perga in Pamphylia; and John, departing from them, returned to Jerusalem. 14But when they departed from Perga, they came to Antioch in Pisidia, and went into the synagogue on the Sabbath day and sat down. 15And after the reading of the Law and the Prophets, the rulers of the synagogue sent to them, saying, "Men *and* brethren, if you have any word of exhortation for the people, say on."

16Then Paul stood up, and motioning with *his* hand said, "Men of Israel, and you who fear God, listen: 17The God of this people Israel[a] chose our fathers, and exalted the people when they dwelt as strangers in the land of Egypt, and with an uplifted arm He brought them out of it. 18Now for a time of about forty years He put up with their ways in the wilderness. 19And when He had destroyed seven nations in the land of Canaan, He distributed their land to them by allotment.

20"After that He gave *them* judges for about four hundred and fifty years, until Samuel the prophet. 21And afterward they asked for a king; so God gave them Saul the son of Kish, a man of the tribe of Benjamin, for forty years. 22And when He had removed him, He raised up for them David as king, to whom also He gave testimony and said, 'I have found David[a] the *son* of Jesse, a man after

My *own* heart, who will do all My will.[b] 23From this man's seed, according to *the* promise, God raised up for Israel a Savior—Jesus—[a] 24after John had first preached, before His coming, the baptism of repentance to all the people of Israel. 25And as John was finishing his course, he said, 'Who do you think I am? I am not *He*. But behold, there comes One after me, the sandals of whose feet I am not worthy to loose.'

26"Men *and* brethren, sons of the family of Abraham, and those among you who fear God, to you the word of this salvation has been sent. 27For those who dwell in Jerusalem, and their rulers, because they did not know Him, nor even the voices of the Prophets which are read every Sabbath, have fulfilled *them* in condemning *Him*. 28And though they found no cause for death *in Him*, they asked Pilate that He should be put to death. 29Now when they had fulfilled all that was written concerning Him, they took *Him* down from the tree and laid *Him* in a tomb. 30But God raised Him from the dead. 31He was seen for many days by those who came up with Him from Galilee to Jerusalem, who are His witnesses to the people. 32And we declare to you glad tidings—that promise which was made to the fathers. 33God has fulfilled this for us their children, in that He has raised up Jesus. As it is also written in the second Psalm:

13:17 [a] M-Text omits *Israel.*   13:22 [a] Psalm 89:20   [b] 1 Samuel 13:14   13:23 [a] M-Text reads *for Israel salvation.*

'You are My Son,
Today I have begotten You.'*a*

34And that He raised Him from the dead, no more to return to corruption, He has spoken thus:

'I will give you the sure mercies of David.'*a*

35Therefore He also says in another *Psalm:*

'You will not allow Your Holy One to see corruption.'*a*

36For David, after he had served his own generation by the will of God, fell asleep, was buried with his fathers, and saw corruption; 37but He whom God raised up saw no corruption. 38Therefore let it be known to you, brethren, that through this Man is preached to you the forgiveness of sins; 39and by Him everyone who believes is justified from all things from which you could not be justified by the law of Moses. 40Beware therefore, lest what has been spoken in the prophets come upon you:

41 'Behold, you despisers,
    Marvel and perish!
For I work a work in your days,
A work which you will by no means believe,
    Though one were to declare it to you.'"[a]

BLESSING AND CONFLICT AT ANTIOCH

42So when the Jews went out of the synagogue,[a] the Gentiles begged that these words might be preached to them the next Sabbath. 43Now when the congregation had broken up, many of the Jews and devout proselytes followed Paul and Barnabas, who, speaking to them, persuaded them to continue in the grace of God.

44On the next Sabbath almost the whole city came together to hear the word of God. 45But when the Jews saw the multitudes, they were filled with envy; and contradicting and blaspheming, they opposed the things spoken by Paul. 46Then Paul and Barnabas grew bold and said, "It was necessary that the word of God should be spoken to you first; but since you reject it, and judge yourselves unworthy of everlasting life, behold, we turn to the Gentiles. 47For so the Lord has commanded us:

13:33 [a] Psalm 2:7   13:34 [a] Isaiah 55:3   13:35 [a] Psalm 16:10   13:41 [a] Habakkuk 1:5   13:42 [a] Or And when they went out, they begged.   when they went out of the synagogue of the Jews; NU-Text reads And when they went out, they begged.

'I have set you as a light to the Gentiles,
That you should be for salvation to
the ends of the earth.'"ᵃ

⁴⁸Now when the Gentiles heard this, they were glad and glorified the word of the Lord. And as many as had been appointed to eternal life believed. ⁴⁹And the word of the Lord was being spread throughout all the region. ⁵⁰But the Jews stirred up the devout and prominent women and the chief men of the city, raised up persecution against Paul and Barnabas, and expelled them from their region. ⁵¹But they shook off the dust from their feet against them, and came to Iconium. ⁵²And the disciples were filled with joy and with the Holy Spirit.

AT ICONIUM

14 Now it happened in Iconium that they went together to the synagogue of the Jews, and so spoke that a great multitude both of the Jews and of the Greeks believed. ²But the unbelieving Jews stirred up the Gentiles and poisoned their minds against the brethren. ³Therefore they stayed there a long time, speaking boldly in the Lord, who was bearing witness to the word of His grace, granting signs and wonders to be done by their hands.

⁴But the multitude of the city was divided: part sided with the Jews, and part with the apostles. ⁵And when a violent attempt was made by both the Gentiles and Jews, with their rulers, to abuse and stone them, ⁶they became aware of it and fled to Lystra and Derbe, cities of Lycaonia, and to the surrounding region. ⁷And they were preaching the gospel there.

IDOLATRY AT LYSTRA

⁸And in Lystra a certain man without strength in his feet was sitting, a cripple from his mother's womb, who had never walked. ⁹This man heard Paul speaking. Paul, observing him intently and seeing that he had faith to be healed, ¹⁰said with a loud voice, "Stand up straight on your feet!" And he leaped and walked. ¹¹Now when the people saw what Paul had done, they raised their voices, saying in the Lycaonian language, "The gods have come down to us in the likeness of men!" ¹²And Barnabas they called Zeus, and Paul, Hermes, because he was the chief speaker. ¹³Then the priest of Zeus, whose temple was in front of the city, brought oxen and garlands to the gates, intending to sacrifice with the multitudes.

¹⁴But when the apostles Barnabas and Paul heard this, they tore their clothes and ran in among the multitude, crying out ¹⁵and saying, "Men, why are you

13:47 ª Isaiah 49:6

doing these things? We also are men with the same nature as you, and preach to you that you should turn from these useless things to the living God, who made the heaven, the earth, the sea, and all things that are in them, ¹⁶who in bygone generations allowed all nations to walk in their own ways. ¹⁷Nevertheless He did not leave Himself without witness, in that He did good, gave us rain from heaven and fruitful seasons, filling our hearts with food and gladness." ¹⁸And with these sayings they could scarcely restrain the multitudes from sacrificing to them.

STONING, ESCAPE TO DERBE

¹⁹Then Jews from Antioch and Iconium came there; and having persuaded the multitudes, they stoned Paul *and* dragged *him* out of the city, supposing him to be dead. ²⁰However, when the disciples gathered around him, he rose up and went into the city. And the next day he departed with Barnabas to Derbe.

STRENGTHENING THE CONVERTS

²¹And when they had preached the gospel to that city and made many disciples, they returned to Lystra, Iconium, and Antioch, ²²strengthening the souls of the disciples, exhorting *them* to continue in the faith, and *saying,* "We must through many tribulations enter the kingdom of God." ²³So when they had appointed

elders in every church, and prayed with fasting, they commended them to the Lord in whom they had believed. 24And after they had passed through Pisidia, they came to Pamphylia. 25Now when they had preached the word in Perga, they went down to Attalia. 26From there they sailed to Antioch, where they had been commended to the grace of God for the work which they had completed.

27Now when they had come and gathered the church together, they reported all that God had done with them, and that He had opened the door of faith to the Gentiles. 28So they stayed there a long time with the disciples.

CONFLICT OVER CIRCUMCISION

15 And certain *men* came down from Judea and taught the brethren, "Unless you are circumcised according to the custom of Moses, you cannot be saved." 2Therefore, when Paul and Barnabas had no small dissension and dispute with them, they determined that Paul and Barnabas and certain others of them should go up to Jerusalem, to the apostles and elders, about this question.

3So, being sent on their way by the church, they passed through Phoenicia and Samaria, describing the conversion of the Gentiles; and they caused great joy to all the brethren. 4And when they had come to Jerusalem, they were received by the church and the apostles and the elders; and they reported all things that God had done with them. 5But some of the sect of the Pharisees who believed rose up, saying, "It is necessary to circumcise them, and to command *them* to keep the law of Moses."

THE JERUSALEM COUNCIL

6Now the apostles and elders came together to consider this matter. 7And when there had been much dispute, Peter rose up *and* said to them: "Men *and* brethren, you know that a good while ago God chose among us, that by my mouth the Gentiles should hear the word of the gospel and believe. 8So God, who knows the heart, acknowledged them by giving them the Holy Spirit, just as *He did* to us, 9and made no distinction between us and them, purifying their hearts by faith. 10Now therefore, why do you test God by putting a yoke on the neck of the disciples which neither our fathers nor we were able to bear? 11But we believe that through the grace of the Lord Jesus Christ*a* we shall be saved in the same manner as they."

12Then all the multitude kept silent and listened to Barnabas and Paul declaring how many miracles and wonders God had worked through them among the Gentiles. 13And after they had become silent, James answered, saying, "Men *and* brethren, listen to me: 14Simon has declared how God at the first visited the Gentiles to take out of them a people for His name. 15And with this the words of the prophets agree, just as it is written:

and elders at Jerusalem. 5So the churches were strengthened in the faith, and increased in number daily.

THE MACEDONIAN CALL

6Now when they had gone through Phrygia and the region of Galatia, they were forbidden by the Holy Spirit to preach the word in Asia. 7After they had come to Mysia, they tried to go into Bithynia, but the Spirit[a] did not permit them. 8So passing by Mysia, they came down to Troas. 9And a vision appeared to Paul in the night. A man of Macedonia stood and pleaded with him, saying, "Come over to Macedonia and help us." 10Now after he had seen the vision, immediately we sought to go to Macedonia, concluding that the Lord had called us to preach the gospel to them.

LYDIA BAPTIZED AT PHILIPPI

11Therefore, sailing from Troas, we ran a straight course to Samothrace, and the next *day* came to Neapolis, 12and from there to Philippi, which is the foremost city of that part of Macedonia, a colony. And we were staying in that city for some days. 13And on the Sabbath day we went out of the city to the riverside, where prayer was customarily made; and we sat down and spoke to the women

16:7 [a] NU-Text adds *of Jesus*.

who met *there.* 14Now a certain woman named Lydia heard *us.* She was a seller of purple from the city of Thyatira, who worshiped God. The Lord opened her heart to heed the things spoken by Paul. 15And when she and her household were baptized, she begged *us,* saying, "If you have judged me to be faithful to the Lord, come to my house and stay." So she persuaded us.

PAUL AND SILAS IMPRISONED

16Now it happened, as we went to prayer, that a certain slave girl possessed with a spirit of divination met us, who brought her masters much profit by fortune-telling. 17This girl followed Paul and us, and cried out, saying, "These men are the servants of the Most High God, who proclaim to us the way of salvation." 18And this she did for many days.

But Paul, greatly annoyed, turned and said to the spirit, "I command you in the name of Jesus Christ to come out of her." And he came out that very hour. 19But when her masters saw that their hope of profit was gone, they seized Paul and Silas and dragged *them* into the marketplace to the authorities.

20And they brought them to the magistrates, and said, "These men, being Jews, exceedingly trouble our city; 21and they teach customs which are not lawful for us, being Romans, to receive or observe." 22Then the multitude rose up together against them; and the magistrates tore off their clothes and commanded *them* to be beaten with rods. 23And when they had laid many stripes on them, they threw *them* into prison, commanding the jailer to keep them securely. 24Having received such a charge, he put them into the inner prison and fastened their feet in the stocks.

THE PHILIPPIAN JAILER SAVED

25But at midnight Paul and Silas were praying and singing hymns to God, and the prisoners were listening to them. 26Suddenly there was a great earthquake, so that the foundations of the prison were shaken; and immediately all the doors were opened and everyone's chains were loosed. 27And the keeper of the prison, awaking from sleep and seeing the prison doors open, supposing the prisoners had fled, drew his sword and was about to kill himself. 28But Paul called with a loud voice, saying, "Do yourself no harm, for we are all here."

29Then he called for a light, ran in, and fell down trembling before Paul and Silas. 30And he brought them out and said, "Sirs, what must I do to be saved?"

31So they said, "Believe on the Lord Jesus Christ, and you will be saved, you and your household." 32Then they spoke the word of the Lord to him and to all who were in his house. 33And he took them the same hour of the night and washed *their* stripes. And immediately he and all his *family* were baptized. ³⁴Now when he had brought them into his house, he set food before them; and he rejoiced, having believed in God with all his household.

PAUL REFUSES TO DEPART SECRETLY

³⁵And when it was day, the magistrates sent the officers, saying, "Let those men go."

³⁶So the keeper of the prison reported these words to Paul, saying, "The magistrates have sent to let you go. Now therefore depart, and go in peace."

³⁷But Paul said to them, "They have beaten us openly, uncondemned Romans, *and* have thrown *us* into prison. And now do they put us out secretly? No indeed! Let them come themselves and get us out."

³⁸And the officers told these words to the magistrates, and they were afraid when they heard that they were Romans. ³⁹Then they came and pleaded with them and brought *them* out, and asked *them* to depart from the city. ⁴⁰So they went out of the prison and entered *the house of* Lydia; and when they had seen the brethren, they encouraged them and departed.

PREACHING CHRIST AT THESSALONICA

17 Now when they had passed through Amphipolis and Apollonia, they came to Thessalonica, where there was a synagogue of the Jews. [2]Then Paul, as his custom was, went in to them, and for three Sabbaths reasoned with them from the Scriptures, [3]explaining and demonstrating that the Christ had to suffer and rise again from the dead, and *saying,* "This Jesus whom I preach to you is the Christ." [4]And some of them were persuaded; and a great multitude of the devout Greeks, and not a few of the leading women, joined Paul and Silas.

ASSAULT ON JASON'S HOUSE

[5]But the Jews who were not persuaded, becoming envious,[a] took some of the evil men from the marketplace, and gathering a mob, set all the city in an uproar and attacked the house of Jason, and sought to bring them out to the people. [6]But when they did not find them, they dragged Jason and some brethren to the rulers of the city, crying out, "These who have turned the world upside down have come here too. [7]Jason has harbored them, and these are all acting contrary to the decrees of Caesar, saying there is another king—Jesus." [8]And they troubled the crowd and the rulers of the city when they heard these things. [9]So when they had taken security from Jason and the rest, they let them go.

17:5 [a] NU-Text omits *who were not persuaded;* M-Text omits *becoming envious.*

MINISTERING AT BEREA

10Then the brethren immediately sent Paul and Silas away by night to Berea. When they arrived, they went into the synagogue of the Jews. 11These were more fair-minded than those in Thessalonica, in that they received the word with all readiness, and searched the Scriptures daily *to find out* whether these things were so. 12Therefore many of them believed, and also not a few of the Greeks, prominent women as well as men. 13But when the Jews from Thessalonica learned that the word of God was preached by Paul at Berea, they came there also and stirred up the crowds. 14Then immediately the brethren sent Paul away, to go to the sea; but both Silas and Timothy remained there. 15So those who conducted Paul brought him to Athens; and receiving a command for Silas and Timothy to come to him with all speed, they departed.

THE PHILOSOPHERS AT ATHENS

16Now while Paul waited for them at Athens, his spirit was provoked within him when he saw that the city was given over to idols. 17Therefore he reasoned in the synagogue with the Jews and with the *Gentile* worshipers, and in the marketplace daily with those who happened to be there. 18Then[a] certain Epicurean and Stoic philosophers encountered him. And some said, "What does this babbler want to say?"

Others said, "He seems to be a proclaimer of foreign gods," because he preached to them Jesus and the resurrection.

19And they took him and brought him to the Areopagus, saying, "May we know what this new doctrine *is* of which you speak? 20For you are bringing some strange things to our ears. Therefore we want to know what these things mean." 21For all the Athenians and the foreigners who were there spent their time in nothing else but either to tell or to hear some new thing.

ADDRESSING THE AREOPAGUS

22Then Paul stood in the midst of the Areopagus and said, "Men of Athens, I perceive that in all things you are very religious; 23for as I was passing through and considering the objects of your worship, I even found an altar with this inscription:

TO THE UNKNOWN GOD.

Therefore, the One whom you worship without knowing, Him I proclaim to you: 24God, who made the world and everything in it, since He is Lord of heaven and

17:18 a NU-Text and M-Text add *also.*

earth, does not dwell in temples made with hands. 25Nor is He worshiped with men's hands, as though He needed anything, since He gives to all life, breath, and all things. 26And He has made from one blood[a] every nation of men to dwell on all the face of the earth, and has determined their preappointed times and the boundaries of their dwellings, 27so that they should seek the Lord, in the hope that they might grope for Him and find Him, though He is not far from each one of us; 28for in Him we live and move and have our being, as also some of your own poets have said, 'For we are also His offspring.' 29Therefore, since we are the offspring of God, we ought not to think that the Divine Nature is like gold or silver or stone, something shaped by art and man's devising. 30Truly, these times of ignorance God overlooked, but now commands all men everywhere to repent, 31because He has appointed a day on which He will judge the world in righteousness by the Man whom He has ordained. He has given assurance of this to all by raising Him from the dead."

32And when they heard of the resurrection of the dead, some mocked, while others said, "We will hear you again on this *matter.*" 33So Paul departed from among them. 34However, some men joined him and believed, among them Dionysius the Areopagite, a woman named Damaris, and others with them.

MINISTERING AT CORINTH

18 After these things Paul departed from Athens and went to Corinth. 2And he found a certain Jew named Aquila, born in Pontus, who had recently come from Italy with his wife Priscilla (because Claudius had commanded all the Jews to depart from Rome); and he came to them. 3So, because he was of the same trade, he stayed with them and worked; for by occupation they were tentmakers. 4And he reasoned in the synagogue every Sabbath, and persuaded both Jews and Greeks.

5When Silas and Timothy had come from Macedonia, Paul was compelled by the Spirit, and testified to the Jews *that* Jesus *is* the Christ. 6But when they opposed him and blasphemed, he shook *his* garments and said to them, "Your blood *be* upon your *own* heads; I *am* clean. From now on I will go to the Gentiles." 7And he departed from there and entered the house of a certain *man* named Justus,*a* *one* who worshiped God, whose house was next door to the synagogue. 8Then Crispus, the ruler of the synagogue, believed on the Lord with all his household. And many of the Corinthians, hearing, believed and were baptized.

9Now the Lord spoke to Paul in the night by a vision, "Do not be afraid, but speak, and do not keep silent; 10for I am with you, and no one will attack you to

17:26 *a* NU-Text omits *blood.*   18:7 *a* NU-Text reads *Titius Justus.*

hurt you; for I have many people in this city." [11]And he continued *there* a year and six months, teaching the word of God among them.

[12]When Gallio was proconsul of Achaia, the Jews with one accord rose up against Paul and brought him to the judgment seat, [13]saying, "This *fellow* persuades men to worship God contrary to the law."

[14]And when Paul was about to open *his* mouth, Gallio said to the Jews, "If it were a matter of wrongdoing or wicked crimes, O Jews, there would be a reason why I should bear with you. [15]But if it is a question of words and names and your own law, look *to it* yourselves; for I do not want to be a judge of such *matters.*" [16]And he drove them from the judgment seat. [17]Then all the Greeks[a] took Sosthenes, the ruler of the synagogue, and beat *him* before the judgment seat. But Gallio took no notice of these things.

PAUL RETURNS TO ANTIOCH

[18]So Paul still remained a good while. Then he took leave of the brethren and sailed for Syria, and Priscilla and Aquila *were* with him. He had *his* hair cut off at Cenchrea, for he had taken a vow. [19]And he came to Ephesus, and left them there; but he himself entered the synagogue and reasoned with the Jews. [20]When they asked *him* to stay a longer time with them, he did not consent, [21]but took

leave of them, saying, "I must by all means keep this coming feast in Jerusalem;[a] but I will return again to you, God willing." And he sailed from Ephesus. [22]And when he had landed at Caesarea, and gone up and greeted the church, he went down to Antioch. [23]After he had spent some time *there*, he departed and went over the region of Galatia and Phrygia in order, strengthening all the disciples.

MINISTRY OF APOLLOS

[24]Now a certain Jew named Apollos, born at Alexandria, an eloquent man *and* mighty in the Scriptures, came to Ephesus. [25]This man had been instructed in the way of the Lord; and being fervent in spirit, he spoke and taught accurately the things of the Lord, though he knew only the baptism of John. [26]So he began to speak boldly in the synagogue. When Aquila and Priscilla heard him, they took him aside and explained to him the way of God more accurately. [27]And when he desired to cross to Achaia, the brethren wrote, exhorting the disciples to receive him; and when he arrived, he greatly helped those who had believed through grace; [28]for he vigorously refuted the Jews publicly, showing from the Scriptures that Jesus is the Christ.

18:17 [a] NU-Text reads *they all.*   18:21 [a] NU-Text omits *I must* through *Jerusalem.*

PAUL AT EPHESUS

19 And it happened, while Apollos was at Corinth, that Paul, having passed through the upper regions, came to Ephesus. And finding some disciples 2he said to them, "Did you receive the Holy Spirit when you believed?"

So they said to him, "We have not so much as heard whether there is a Holy Spirit."

3And he said to them, "Into what then were you baptized?"

So they said, "Into John's baptism."

4Then Paul said, "John indeed baptized with a baptism of repentance, saying to the people that they should believe on Him who would come after him, that is, on Christ Jesus."

5When they heard *this*, they were baptized in the name of the Lord Jesus. 6And when Paul had laid hands on them, the Holy Spirit came upon them, and they spoke with tongues and prophesied. 7Now the men were about twelve in all.

8And he went into the synagogue and spoke boldly for three months, reasoning and persuading concerning the things of the kingdom of God. 9But when some were hardened and did not believe, but spoke evil of the Way before the multitude, he departed from them and withdrew the disciples, reasoning daily in the school of Tyrannus. 10And this continued for two years, so that all who dwelt in Asia heard the word of the Lord Jesus, both Jews and Greeks.

MIRACLES GLORIFY CHRIST

11Now God worked unusual miracles by the hands of Paul, 12so that even handkerchiefs or aprons were brought from his body to the sick, and the diseases left them and the evil spirits went out of them. 13Then some of the itinerant Jewish exorcists took it upon themselves to call the name of the Lord Jesus over those who had evil spirits, saying, "We*a* exorcise you by the Jesus whom Paul preaches." 14Also there were seven sons of Sceva, a Jewish chief priest, who did so.

15And the evil spirit answered and said, "Jesus I know, and Paul I know; but who are you?"

16Then the man in whom the evil spirit was leaped on them, overpowered*a* them, and prevailed against them,*b* so that they fled out of that house naked and wounded. 17This became known both to all Jews and Greeks dwelling in Ephesus; and fear fell on them all, and the name of the Lord Jesus was magnified. 18And many who had believed came confessing and telling their deeds. 19Also, many of those who had practiced magic brought their books together and burned *them* in the sight of all. And they counted up the value of them,

19:13 *a* NU-Text reads I.   19:16 *a* M-Text reads *and they overpowered.*   *b* NU-Text reads *both of them.*

and *it* totaled fifty thousand *pieces* of silver. 20So the word of the Lord grew mightily and prevailed.

THE RIOT AT EPHESUS

21When these things were accomplished, Paul purposed in the Spirit, when he had passed through Macedonia and Achaia, to go to Jerusalem, saying, "After I have been there, I must also see Rome." 22So he sent into Macedonia two of those who ministered to him, Timothy and Erastus, but he himself stayed in Asia for a time.

23And about that time there arose a great commotion about the Way. 24For a certain man named Demetrius, a silversmith, who made silver shrines of Diana,*a* brought no small profit to the craftsmen. 25He called them together with the workers of similar occupation, and said: "Men, you know that we have our prosperity by this trade. 26Moreover you see and hear that not only at Ephesus, but throughout almost all Asia, this Paul has persuaded and turned away many people, saying that they are not gods which are made with hands. 27So not only is this trade of ours in danger of falling into disrepute, but also the temple of the great goddess Diana may be despised and her magnificence destroyed,*a* whom all Asia and the world worship."

28Now when they heard *this*, they were full of wrath and cried out, saying, "Great *is* Diana of the Ephesians!" 29So the whole city was filled with confusion, and rushed into the theater with one accord, having seized Gaius and Aristarchus, Macedonians, Paul's travel companions. 30And when Paul wanted to go in to the people, the disciples would not allow him. 31Then some of the officials of Asia, who were his friends, sent to him pleading that he would not venture into the theater. 32Some therefore cried one thing and some another, for the assembly was confused, and most of them did not know why they had come together. 33And they drew Alexander out of the multitude, the Jews putting him forward. And Alexander motioned with his hand, and wanted to make his defense to the people. 34But when they found out that he was a Jew, all with one voice cried out for about two hours, "Great *is* Diana of the Ephesians!"

35And when the city clerk had quieted the crowd, he said: "Men of Ephesus, what man is there who does not know that the city of the Ephesians is temple guardian of the great goddess Diana, and of the *image* which fell down from Zeus? 36Therefore, since these things cannot be denied, you ought to be quiet and do nothing rashly. 37For you have brought these men here who are neither robbers of temples nor blasphemers of your[a] goddess. 38Therefore, if Demetrius

19:24, [a] Greek *Artemis*   19:27, [a] NU-Text reads *she be deposed from her magnificence.*   19:37, [a] NU-Text reads *our.*

and his fellow craftsmen have a case against anyone, the courts are open and there are proconsuls. Let them bring charges against one another. ³⁹But if you have any other inquiry to make, it shall be determined in the lawful assembly. ⁴⁰For we are in danger of being called in question for today's uproar, there being no reason which we may give to account for this disorderly gathering." ⁴¹And when he had said these things, he dismissed the assembly.

JOURNEYS IN GREECE

20 After the uproar had ceased, Paul called the disciples to *himself*, embraced *them*, and departed to go to Macedonia. ²Now when he had gone over that region and encouraged them with many words, he came to Greece ³and stayed three months. And when the Jews plotted against him as he was about to sail to Syria, he decided to return through Macedonia. ⁴And Sopater of Berea accompanied him to Asia—also Aristarchus and Secundus of the Thessalonians, and Gaius of Derbe, and Timothy, and Tychicus and Trophimus of Asia. ⁵These men, going ahead, waited for us at Troas. ⁶But we sailed away from Philippi after the Days of Unleavened Bread, and in five days joined them at Troas, where we stayed seven days.

MINISTERING AT TROAS

7Now on the first *day* of the week, when the disciples came together to break bread, Paul, ready to depart the next day, spoke to them and continued his message until midnight. 8There were many lamps in the upper room where they[a] were gathered together. 9And in a window sat a certain young man named Eutychus, who was sinking into a deep sleep. He was overcome by sleep; and as Paul continued speaking, he fell down from the third story and was taken up dead. 10But Paul went down, fell on him, and embracing *him* said, "Do not trouble yourselves, for his life is in him." 11Now when he had come up, had broken bread and eaten, and talked a long while, even till daybreak, he departed. 12And they brought the young man in alive, and they were not a little comforted.

FROM TROAS TO MILETUS

13Then we went ahead to the ship and sailed to Assos, there intending to take Paul on board; for so he had given orders, intending himself to go on foot. 14And when he met us at Assos, we took him on board and came to Mitylene. 15We sailed from there, and the next *day* came opposite Chios. The following *day* we arrived at Samos and stayed at Trogyllium. The next *day* we came to Miletus. 16For Paul had decided to sail past Ephesus, so that he would not have

20:8 a NU-Text and M-Text read *we*.

to spend time in Asia; for he was hurrying to be at Jerusalem, if possible, on the Day of Pentecost.

THE EPHESIAN ELDERS EXHORTED

17From Miletus he sent to Ephesus and called for the elders of the church. 18And when they had come to him, he said to them: "You know, from the first day that I came to Asia, in what manner I always lived among you, 19serving the Lord with all humility, with many tears and trials which happened to me by the plotting of the Jews; 20how I kept back nothing that was helpful, but proclaimed it to you, and taught you publicly and from house to house, 21testifying to Jews, and also to Greeks, repentance toward God and faith toward our Lord Jesus Christ. 22And see, now I go bound in the spirit to Jerusalem, not knowing the things that will happen to me there, 23except that the Holy Spirit testifies in every city, saying that chains and tribulations await me. 24But none of these things move me; nor do I count my life dear to myself,[a] so that I may finish my race with joy, and the ministry which I received from the Lord Jesus, to testify to the gospel of the grace of God.

25"And indeed, now I know that you all, among whom I have gone preaching the kingdom of God, will see my face no more. 26Therefore I testify to you this day that I *am* innocent of the blood of all *men*. [27]For I have not shunned to declare to you the whole counsel of God. [28]Therefore take heed to yourselves and to all the flock, among which the Holy Spirit has made you overseers, to shepherd the church of God[a] which He purchased with His own blood. [29]For I know this, that after my departure savage wolves will come in among you, not sparing the flock. [30]Also from among yourselves men will rise up, speaking perverse things, to draw away the disciples after themselves. [31]Therefore watch, and remember that for three years I did not cease to warn everyone night and day with tears.

[32]"So now, brethren, I commend you to God and to the word of His grace, which is able to build you up and give you an inheritance among all those who are sanctified. [33]I have coveted no one's silver or gold or apparel. [34]Yes,[a] you yourselves know that these hands have provided for my necessities, and for those who were with me. [35]I have shown you in every way, by laboring like this, that you must support the weak. And remember the words of the Lord Jesus, that He said, 'It is more blessed to give than to receive.'"

[36]And when he had said these things, he knelt down and prayed with them all. [37]Then they all wept freely, and fell on Paul's neck and kissed him, [38]sorrowing

20:24 [a] NU-Text reads *But I do not count my life of any value or dear to myself.*   20:28 [a] NU-Text reads *of the Lord and God.*   20:34 [a] NU-Text and M-Text omit *Yes.*

most of all for the words which he spoke, that they would see his face no more. And they accompanied him to the ship.

WARNINGS ON THE JOURNEY TO JERUSALEM

21 Now it came to pass, that when we had departed from them and set sail, running a straight course we came to Cos, the following *day* to Rhodes, and from there to Patara. [2] And finding a ship sailing over to Phoenicia, we went aboard and set sail. [3] When we had sighted Cyprus, we passed it on the left, sailed to Syria, and landed at Tyre; for there the ship was to unload her cargo. [4] And finding disciples,[a] we stayed there seven days. They told Paul through the Spirit not to go up to Jerusalem. [5] When we had come to the end of those days, we departed and went on our way; and they all accompanied us, with wives and children, till *we were* out of the city. And we knelt down on the shore and prayed. [6] When we had taken our leave of one another, we boarded the ship, and they returned home.

[7] And when we had finished *our* voyage from Tyre, we came to Ptolemais, greeted the brethren, and stayed with them one day. [8] On the next *day* we who were Paul's companions[a] departed and came to Caesarea, and entered the house of Philip the evangelist, who was *one* of the seven, and stayed with him. [9] Now

this man had four virgin daughters who prophesied. [10] And as we stayed many days, a certain prophet named Agabus came down from Judea. [11] When he had come to us, he took Paul's belt, bound his *own* hands and feet, and said, "Thus says the Holy Spirit, 'So shall the Jews at Jerusalem bind the man who owns this belt, and deliver *him* into the hands of the Gentiles.'"

[12] Now when we heard these things, both we and those from that place pleaded with him not to go up to Jerusalem. [13] Then Paul answered, "What do you mean by weeping and breaking my heart? For I am ready not only to be bound, but also to die at Jerusalem for the name of the Lord Jesus."

[14] So when he would not be persuaded, we ceased, saying, "The will of the Lord be done."

PAUL URGED TO MAKE PEACE

[15] And after those days we packed and went up to Jerusalem. [16] Also some of the disciples from Caesarea went with us and brought with them a certain Mnason of Cyprus, an early disciple, with whom we were to lodge.

[17] And when we had come to Jerusalem, the brethren received us gladly. [18] On the following *day* Paul went in with us to James, and all the elders were present. [19] When he had greeted them, he told in detail those things which God had

21:4 [a] NU-Text reads *the disciples.*   21:8 [a] NU-Text omits *who were Paul's companions.*

done among the Gentiles through his ministry. 20And when they heard *it*, they glorified the Lord. And they said to him, "You see, brother, how many myriads of Jews there are who have believed, and they are all zealous for the law; 21but they have been informed about you that you teach all the Jews who are among the Gentiles to forsake Moses, saying that they ought not to circumcise *their* children nor to walk according to the customs. 22What then? The assembly must certainly meet, for they willᵃ hear that you have come. 23Therefore do what we tell you: We have four men who have taken a vow. 24Take them and be purified with them, and pay their expenses so that they may shave *their* heads, and that all may know that those things of which they were informed concerning you are nothing, but *that* you yourself also walk orderly and keep the law. 25But concerning the Gentiles who believe, we have written *and* decided that they should observe no such thing, exceptᵃ that they should keep themselves from *things* offered to idols, from blood, from things strangled, and from sexual immorality."

ARRESTED IN THE TEMPLE

26Then Paul took the men, and the next day, having been purified with them, entered the temple to announce the expiration of the days of purification, at which time an offering should be made for each one of them.

that he should be examined under scourging, so that he might know why they shouted so against him. 25And as they bound him with thongs, Paul said to the centurion who stood by, "Is it lawful for you to scourge a man who is a Roman, and uncondemned?"

26When the centurion heard *that*, he went and told the commander, saying, "Take care what you do, for this man is a Roman."

27Then the commander came and said to him, "Tell me, are you a Roman?"
He said, "Yes."

28The commander answered, "With a large sum I obtained this citizenship."
And Paul said, "But I was born *a citizen*."

29Then immediately those who were about to examine him withdrew from him; and the commander was also afraid after he found out that he was a Roman, and because he had bound him.

THE SANHEDRIN DIVIDED

30The next day, because he wanted to know for certain why he was accused by the Jews, he released him from *his* bonds, and commanded the chief priests and all their council to appear, and brought Paul down and set him before them.

22:20 *a* NU-Text omits *to his death.*

23 Then Paul, looking earnestly at the council, said, "Men *and* brethren, I have lived in all good conscience before God until this day." 2And the high priest Ananias commanded those who stood by him to strike him on the mouth. 3Then Paul said to him, "God will strike you, *you* whitewashed wall! For you sit to judge me according to the law, and do you command me to be struck contrary to the law?"

4And those who stood by said, "Do you revile God's high priest?"

5Then Paul said, "I did not know, brethren, that he was the high priest; for it is written, 'You shall not speak evil of a ruler of your people.'"ᵃ

6But when Paul perceived that one part were Sadducees and the other Pharisees, he cried out in the council, "Men *and* brethren, I am a Pharisee, the son of a Pharisee; concerning the hope and resurrection of the dead I am being judged!"

7And when he had said this, a dissension arose between the Pharisees and the Sadducees; and the assembly was divided. 8For Sadducees say that there is no resurrection—and no angel or spirit; but the Pharisees confess both. 9Then there arose a loud outcry. And the scribes of the Pharisees' party arose and protested, saying, "We find no evil in this man; but if a spirit or an angel has spoken to him, let us not fight against God."ᵃ

10Now when there arose a great dissension, the commander, fearing lest Paul might be pulled to pieces by them, commanded the soldiers to go down and take him by force from among them, and bring *him* into the barracks.

THE PLOT AGAINST PAUL

¹¹But the following night the Lord stood by him and said, "Be of good cheer, Paul; for as you have testified for Me in Jerusalem, so you must also bear witness at Rome."

¹²And when it was day, some of the Jews banded together and bound themselves under an oath, saying that they would neither eat nor drink till they had killed Paul. ¹³Now there were more than forty who had formed this conspiracy. ¹⁴They came to the chief priests and elders, and said, "We have bound ourselves under a great oath that we will eat nothing until we have killed Paul. ¹⁵Now you, therefore, together with the council, suggest to the commander that he be brought down to you tomorrow,ᵃ as though you were going to make further inquiries concerning him; but we are ready to kill him before he comes near."

¹⁶So when Paul's sister's son heard of their ambush, he went and entered the barracks and told Paul. ¹⁷Then Paul called one of the centurions to *him* and said, "Take this young man to the commander, for he has something to

23:5 ᵃ Exodus 22:28   23:9 ᵃ NU-Text omits last clause and reads *what if a spirit or an angel has spoken to him?*   23:15 ᵃ NU-Text omits *tomorrow.*

tell him." ¹⁸So he took him and brought *him* to the commander and said, "Paul the prisoner called me to *him* and asked *me* to bring this young man to you. He has something to say to you."

¹⁹Then the commander took him by the hand, went aside, and asked privately, "What is it that you have to tell me?"

²⁰And he said, "The Jews have agreed to ask that you bring Paul down to the council tomorrow, as though they were going to inquire more fully about him. ²¹But do not yield to them, for more than forty of them lie in wait for him, men who have bound themselves by an oath that they will neither eat nor drink till they have killed him; and now they are ready, waiting for the promise from you."

²²So the commander let the young man depart, and commanded *him*, "Tell no one that you have revealed these things to me."

SENT TO FELIX

²³And he called for two centurions, saying, "Prepare two hundred soldiers, seventy horsemen, and two hundred spearmen to go to Caesarea at the third hour of the night; ²⁴and provide mounts to set Paul on, and bring *him* safely to Felix the governor." ²⁵He wrote a letter in the following manner:

26 Claudius Lysias,

To the most excellent governor Felix:

Greetings.

27 This man was seized by the Jews and was about to be killed by them. Coming with the troops I rescued him, having learned that he was a Roman. 28And when I wanted to know the reason they accused him, I brought him before their council. 29I found out that he was accused concerning questions of their law, but had nothing charged against him deserving of death or chains. 30And when it was told me that the Jews lay in wait for the man,[a] I sent him immediately to you, and also commanded his accusers to state before you the charges against him.

Farewell.

31Then the soldiers, as they were commanded, took Paul and brought *him* by night to Antipatris. 32The next day they left the horsemen to go on with him, and

23:30 [a] NU-Text reads *there would be a plot against the man.*

returned to the barracks. 33When they came to Caesarea and had delivered the letter to the governor, they also presented Paul to him. 34And when the governor had read *it*, he asked what province he was from. And when he understood that *he was* from Cilicia, 35he said, "I will hear you when your accusers also have come." And he commanded him to be kept in Herod's Praetorium.

ACCUSED OF SEDITION

24 Now after five days Ananias the high priest came down with the elders and a certain orator *named* Tertullus. These gave evidence to the governor against Paul.

2And when he was called upon, Tertullus began his accusation, saying: "Seeing that through you we enjoy great peace, and prosperity is being brought to this nation by your foresight, 3we accept *it* always and in all places, most noble Felix, with all thankfulness. 4Nevertheless, not to be tedious to you any further, I beg you to hear, by your courtesy, a few words from us. 5For we have found this man a plague, a creator of dissension among all the Jews throughout the world, and a ringleader of the sect of the Nazarenes. 6He even tried to profane the temple, and we seized him,[a] and wanted to judge him according to our law. 7But the commander Lysias came by and with great violence took *him* out of our hands, 8commanding his accusers to come to you. By examining him yourself you may ascertain all these things of which we accuse him." 9And the Jews also assented,^{a} maintaining that these things were so.

THE DEFENSE BEFORE FELIX

10Then Paul, after the governor had nodded to him to speak, answered: "Inasmuch as I know that you have been for many years a judge of this nation, I do the more cheerfully answer for myself, 11because you may ascertain that it is no more than twelve days since I went up to Jerusalem to worship. 12And they neither found me in the temple disputing with anyone nor inciting the crowd, either in the synagogues or in the city. 13Nor can they prove the things of which they now accuse me. 14But this I confess to you, that according to the Way which they call a sect, so I worship the God of my fathers, believing all things which are written in the Law and in the Prophets. 15I have hope in God, which they themselves also accept, that there will be a resurrection of the dead,^{a} both of the just and the unjust. 16This being so, I myself always strive to have a conscience without offense toward God and men.

17"Now after many years I came to bring alms and offerings to my nation,

24:6 ^{a} NU-Text ends the sentence here and omits the rest of verse 6, all of verse 7, and the first clause of verse 8.   24:9 ^{a} NU-Text and M-Text read joined the attack.   24:15 ^{a} NU-Text omits of the dead.

18in the midst of which some Jews from Asia found me purified in the temple, neither with a mob nor with tumult. 19They ought to have been here before you to object if they had anything against me. 20Or else let those who are *here* themselves say if they found any wrongdoing*a* in me while I stood before the council, 21unless *it is* for this one statement which I cried out, standing among them, "Concerning the resurrection of the dead I am being judged by you this day.'"

FELIX PROCRASTINATES

22But when Felix heard these things, having more accurate knowledge of *the* Way, he adjourned the proceedings and said, "When Lysias the commander comes down, I will make a decision on your case." 23So he commanded the centurion to keep Paul and to let *him* have liberty, and told him not to forbid any of his friends to provide for or visit him.

24And after some days, when Felix came with his wife Drusilla, who was Jewish, he sent for Paul and heard him concerning the faith in Christ. 25Now as he reasoned about righteousness, self-control, and the judgment to come, Felix was afraid and answered, "Go away for now; when I have a convenient time I will call for you." 26Meanwhile he also hoped that money would be given him by Paul, that he might release him.[a] Therefore he sent for him more often and conversed with him.

27But after two years Porcius Festus succeeded Felix; and Felix, wanting to do the Jews a favor, left Paul bound.

PAUL APPEALS TO CAESAR

25 Now when Festus had come to the province, after three days he went up from Caesarea to Jerusalem. 2Then the high priest[a] and the chief men of the Jews informed him against Paul; and they petitioned him, 3asking a favor against him, that he would summon him to Jerusalem—while *they* lay in ambush along the road to kill him. 4But Festus answered that Paul should be kept at Caesarea, and that he himself was going *there* shortly. 5"Therefore," he said, "let those who have authority among you go down with *me* and accuse this man, to see if there is any fault in him."

6And when he had remained among them more than ten days, he went down to Caesarea. And the next day, sitting on the judgment seat, he commanded Paul to be brought. 7When he had come, the Jews who had come down from Jerusalem stood about and laid many serious complaints against Paul, which they could

24:20 [a] NU-Text and M-Text read *say what wrongdoing they found.* 24:26 [a] NU-Text omits *that he might release him.* 25:2 [a] NU-Text reads *chief priests.*

not prove, [8]while he answered for himself, "Neither against the law of the Jews, nor against the temple, nor against Caesar have I offended in anything at all."

[9]But Festus, wanting to do the Jews a favor, answered Paul and said, "Are you willing to go up to Jerusalem and there be judged before me concerning these things?"

[10]So Paul said, "I stand at Caesar's judgment seat, where I ought to be judged. To the Jews I have done no wrong, as you very well know. [11]For if I am an offender, or have committed anything deserving of death, I do not object to dying; but if there is nothing in these things of which these men accuse me, no one can deliver me to them. I appeal to Caesar."

[12]Then Festus, when he had conferred with the council, answered, "You have appealed to Caesar? To Caesar you shall go!"

PAUL BEFORE AGRIPPA

[13]And after some days King Agrippa and Bernice came to Caesarea to greet Festus. [14]When they had been there many days, Festus laid Paul's case before the king, saying: "There is a certain man left a prisoner by Felix, [15]about whom the chief priests and the elders of the Jews informed *me*, when I was in Jerusalem, asking for a judgment against him. [16]To them I answered, 'It is not the custom

of the Romans to deliver any man to destruction[a] before the accused meets the accusers face to face, and has opportunity to answer for himself concerning the charge against him.' [17]Therefore when they had come together, without any delay, the next day I sat on the judgment seat and commanded the man to be brought in. [18]When the accusers stood up, they brought no accusation against him of such things as I supposed, [19]but had some questions against him about their own religion and about a certain Jesus, who had died, whom Paul affirmed to be alive. [20]And because I was uncertain of such questions, I asked whether he was willing to go to Jerusalem and there be judged concerning these matters. [21]But when Paul appealed to be reserved for the decision of Augustus, I commanded him to be kept till I could send him to Caesar."

[22]Then Agrippa said to Festus, "I also would like to hear the man myself."

"Tomorrow," he said, "you shall hear him."

[23]So the next day, when Agrippa and Bernice had come with great pomp, and had entered the auditorium with the commanders and the prominent men of the city, at Festus' command Paul was brought in. [24]And Festus said: "King Agrippa and all the men who are here present with us, you see this man about whom the whole assembly of the Jews petitioned me, both at Jerusalem and here, crying out that he was not fit to live any longer. [25]But when I found that he

25:16 [a] NU-Text omits to destruction, although it is implied.

had committed nothing deserving of death, and that he himself had appealed to Augustus, I decided to send him. ²⁶I have nothing certain to write to my lord concerning him. Therefore I have brought him out before you, and especially before you, King Agrippa, so that after the examination has taken place I may have something to write. ²⁷For it seems to me unreasonable to send a prisoner and not to specify the charges against him."

PAUL'S EARLY LIFE

26 Then Agrippa said to Paul, "You are permitted to speak for yourself."
So Paul stretched out his hand and answered for himself: ²"I think myself happy, King Agrippa, because today I shall answer for myself before you concerning all the things of which I am accused by the Jews, ³especially because you are expert in all customs and questions which have to do with the Jews. Therefore I beg you to hear me patiently.

⁴"My manner of life from my youth, which was spent from the beginning among my own nation at Jerusalem, all the Jews know. ⁵They knew me from the first, if they were willing to testify, that according to the strictest sect of our religion I lived a Pharisee. ⁶And now I stand and am judged for the hope of the promise made by God to our fathers. ⁷To this *promise* our twelve tribes,

earnestly serving *God* night and day, hope to attain. For this hope's sake, King Agrippa, I am accused by the Jews. 8Why should it be thought incredible by you that God raises the dead?

9"Indeed, I myself thought I must do many things contrary to the name of Jesus of Nazareth. 10This I also did in Jerusalem, and many of the saints I shut up in prison, having received authority from the chief priests; and when they were put to death, I cast my vote against *them.* 11And I punished them often in every synagogue and compelled *them* to blaspheme; and being exceedingly enraged against them, I persecuted *them* even to foreign cities.

PAUL RECOUNTS HIS CONVERSION

12"While thus occupied, as I journeyed to Damascus with authority and commission from the chief priests, 13at midday, O king, along the road I saw a light from heaven, brighter than the sun, shining around me and those who journeyed with me. 14And when we all had fallen to the ground, I heard a voice speaking to me and saying in the Hebrew language, 'Saul, Saul, why are you persecuting Me? *It is* hard for you to kick against the goads.' 15So I said, 'Who are You, Lord?' And He said, 'I am Jesus, whom you are persecuting. 16But rise and stand on your feet; for I have appeared to you for this purpose, to make you a minister and a witness both of the things which you have seen and of the things which I will yet reveal to you. 17I will deliver you from the *Jewish* people, as well as *from* the Gentiles, to whom I now[a] send you, 18to open their eyes, *in order* to turn *them* from darkness to light, and *from* the power of Satan to God, that they may receive forgiveness of sins and an inheritance among those who are sanctified by faith in Me.'

PAUL'S POST-CONVERSION LIFE

19"Therefore, King Agrippa, I was not disobedient to the heavenly vision, 20but declared first to those in Damascus and in Jerusalem, and throughout all the region of Judea, and *then* to the Gentiles, that they should repent, turn to God, and do works befitting repentance. 21For these reasons the Jews seized me in the temple and tried to kill *me.* 22Therefore, having obtained help from God, to this day I stand, witnessing both to small and great, saying no other things than those which the prophets and Moses said would come— 23that the Christ would suffer, that He would be the first to rise from the dead, and would proclaim light to the *Jewish* people and to the Gentiles."

AGRIPPA PARRIES PAUL'S CHALLENGE

24Now as he thus made his defense, Festus said with a loud voice, "Paul, you are beside yourself! Much learning is driving you mad!"

25But he said, "I am not mad, most noble Festus, but speak the words of truth and reason. 26For the king, before whom I also speak freely, knows these things; for I am convinced that none of these things escapes his attention, since this thing was not done in a corner. 27King Agrippa, do you believe the prophets? I know that you do believe."

28Then Agrippa said to Paul, "You almost persuade me to become a Christian."

29And Paul said, "I would to God that not only you, but also all who hear me today, might become both almost and altogether such as I am, except for these chains."

30When he had said these things, the king stood up, as well as the governor and Bernice and those who sat with them; 31and when they had gone aside, they talked among themselves, saying, "This man is doing nothing deserving of death or chains."

32Then Agrippa said to Festus, "This man might have been set free if he had not appealed to Caesar."

THE VOYAGE TO ROME BEGINS

27 And when it was decided that we should sail to Italy, they delivered Paul and some other prisoners to *one* named Julius, a centurion of the Augustan

26:17 *a* NU-Text and M-Text omit *now.*

Regiment. 2So, entering a ship of Adramyttium, we put to sail along the coasts of Asia. Aristarchus, a Macedonian of Thessalonica, was with us. 3And the next *day* we landed at Sidon. And Julius treated Paul kindly and gave *him* liberty to go to his friends and receive care. 4When we had put to sea from there, we sailed under *the shelter of* Cyprus, because the winds were contrary. 5And when we had sailed over the sea which is off Cilicia and Pamphylia, we came to Myra, *a city* of Lycia. 6There the centurion found an Alexandrian ship sailing to Italy, and he put us on board.

7When we had sailed slowly many days, and arrived with difficulty off Cnidus, the wind not permitting us to proceed, we sailed under *the shelter of* Crete off Salmone. 8Passing it with difficulty, we came to a place called Fair Havens, near the city of Lasea.

PAUL'S WARNING IGNORED

9Now when much time had been spent, and sailing *was* now dangerous because the Fast was already over, Paul advised them, 10saying, "Men, I perceive that this voyage will end with disaster and much loss, not only of the cargo and ship, but also our lives." 11Nevertheless the centurion was more persuaded by the helmsman and the owner of the ship than by the things spoken by Paul.

12And because the harbor was not suitable to winter in, the majority advised to set sail from there also, if by any means they could reach Phoenix, a harbor of Crete opening toward the southwest and northwest, *and* winter *there.*

IN THE TEMPEST

13When the south wind blew softly, supposing that they had obtained *their* desire, putting out to sea, they sailed close by Crete. 14But not long after, a tempestuous head wind arose, called Euroclydon.[a] 15So when the ship was caught, and could not head into the wind, we let *her* drive. 16And running under *the shelter of* an island called Clauda,[a] we secured the skiff with difficulty. 17When they had taken it on board, they used cables to undergird the ship; and fearing lest they should run aground on the Syrtis[a] *Sands,* they struck sail and so were driven. 18And because we were exceedingly tempest-tossed, the next *day* they lightened the ship. 19On the third *day* we threw the ship's tackle overboard with our own hands. 20Now when neither sun nor stars appeared for many days, and no small tempest beat on *us,* all hope that we would be saved was finally given up.

21But after long abstinence from food, then Paul stood in the midst of them and said, "Men, you should have listened to me, and not have sailed from Crete

27:14 [a] NU-Text reads *Euraquilon.*   27:16 [a] NU-Text reads *Cauda.*   27:17 [a] M-Text reads *Syrtes.*

and incurred this disaster and loss. 22And now I urge you to take heart, for there will be no loss of life among you, but only of the ship. 23For there stood by me this night an angel of the God to whom I belong and whom I serve, 24saying, 'Do not be afraid, Paul; you must be brought before Caesar; and indeed God has granted you all those who sail with you.' 25Therefore take heart, men, for I believe God that it will be just as it was told me. 26However, we must run aground on a certain island."

27Now when the fourteenth night had come, as we were driven up and down in the Adriatic *Sea*, about midnight the sailors sensed that they were drawing near some land. 28And they took soundings and found *it* to be twenty fathoms; and when they had gone a little farther, they took soundings again and found *it* to be fifteen fathoms. 29Then, fearing lest we should run aground on the rocks, they dropped four anchors from the stern, and prayed for day to come. 30And as the sailors were seeking to escape from the ship, when they had let down the skiff into the sea, under pretense of putting out anchors from the prow, 31Paul said to the centurion and the soldiers, "Unless these men stay in the ship, you cannot be saved." 32Then the soldiers cut away the ropes of the skiff and let it fall off.

33And as day was about to dawn, Paul implored *them* all to take food, saying,

"Today is the fourteenth day you have waited and continued without food, and eaten nothing. 34Therefore I urge you to take nourishment, for this is for your survival, since not a hair will fall from the head of any of you." 35And when he had said these things, he took bread and gave thanks to God in the presence of them all; and when he had broken *it* he began to eat. 36Then they were all encouraged, and also took food themselves. 37And in all we were two hundred and seventy-six persons on the ship. 38So when they had eaten enough, they lightened the ship and threw out the wheat into the sea.

SHIPWRECKED ON MALTA

39When it was day, they did not recognize the land; but they observed a bay with a beach, onto which they planned to run the ship if possible. 40And they let go the anchors and left *them* in the sea, meanwhile loosing the rudder ropes; and they hoisted the mainsail to the wind and made for shore. 41But striking a place where two seas met, they ran the ship aground; and the prow stuck fast and remained immovable, but the stern was being broken up by the violence of the waves.

42And the soldiers' plan was to kill the prisoners, lest any of them should swim away and escape. 43But the centurion, wanting to save Paul, kept them from *their* purpose, and commanded that those who could swim should jump *overboard* first and get to land, 44and the rest, some on boards and some on *parts* of the ship. And so it was that they all escaped safely to land.

PAUL'S MINISTRY ON MALTA

28 Now when they had escaped, they then found out that the island was called Malta. 2And the natives showed us unusual kindness; for they kindled a fire and made us all welcome, because of the rain that was falling and because of the cold. 3But when Paul had gathered a bundle of sticks and laid *them* on the fire, a viper came out because of the heat, and fastened on his hand. 4So when the natives saw the creature hanging from his hand, they said to one another, "No doubt this man is a murderer, whom, though he has escaped the sea, yet justice does not allow to live." 5But he shook off the creature into the fire and suffered no harm. 6However, they were expecting that he would swell up or suddenly fall down dead. But after they had looked for a long time and saw no harm come to him, they changed their minds and said that he was a god.

7In that region there was an estate of the leading citizen of the island, whose name was Publius, who received us and entertained us courteously for three days. 8And it happened that the father of Publius lay sick of a fever and dysentery. Paul went in to him and prayed, and he laid his hands on him and healed him. ⁹So when this was done, the rest of those on the island who had diseases also came and were healed. ¹⁰They also honored us in many ways; and when we departed, they provided such things as were necessary.

ARRIVAL AT ROME

¹¹After three months we sailed in an Alexandrian ship whose figurehead was the Twin Brothers, which had wintered at the island. ¹²And landing at Syracuse, we stayed three days. ¹³From there we circled round and reached Rhegium. And after one day the south wind blew; and the next day we came to Puteoli, ¹⁴where we found brethren, and were invited to stay with them seven days. And so we went toward Rome. ¹⁵And from there, when the brethren heard about us, they came to meet us as far as Appii Forum and Three Inns. When Paul saw them, he thanked God and took courage.

¹⁶Now when we came to Rome, the centurion delivered the prisoners to the captain of the guard; but Paul was permitted to dwell by himself with the soldier who guarded him.

PAUL'S MINISTRY AT ROME

¹⁷And it came to pass after three days that Paul called the leaders of the Jews together. So when they had come together, he said to them: "Men *and* brethren,

though I have done nothing against our people or the customs of our fathers, yet I was delivered as a prisoner from Jerusalem into the hands of the Romans, 18who, when they had examined me, wanted to let *me* go, because there was no cause for putting me to death. 19But when the Jews[a] spoke against *it*, I was compelled to appeal to Caesar, not that I had anything of which to accuse my nation. 20For this reason therefore I have called for you, to see *you* and speak with *you*, because for the hope of Israel I am bound with this chain."

21Then they said to him, "We neither received letters from Judea concerning you, nor have any of the brethren who came reported or spoken any evil of you. 22But we desire to hear from you what you think; for concerning this sect, we know that it is spoken against everywhere."

23So when they had appointed him a day, many came to him at *his* lodging, to whom he explained and solemnly testified of the kingdom of God, persuading them concerning Jesus from both the Law of Moses and the Prophets, from morning till evening. 24And some were persuaded by the things which were spoken, and some disbelieved. 25So when they did not agree among themselves, they departed after Paul had said one word: "The Holy Spirit spoke rightly through Isaiah the prophet to our[a] fathers, 26saying,

'Go to this people and say:
"Hearing you will hear, and shall not understand;
    And seeing you will see, and not perceive;
27 For the hearts of this people have grown dull.
    Their ears are hard of hearing,
    And their eyes they have closed,
    Lest they should see with *their* eyes
        and hear with *their* ears,
    Lest they should understand with *their* hearts and turn,
    So that I should heal them."*a*

28"Therefore let it be known to you that the salvation of God has been sent to the Gentiles, and they will hear it!" 29And when he had said these words, the Jews departed and had a great dispute among themselves.*a* 30Then Paul dwelt two whole years in his own rented house, and received all who came to him, 31preaching the kingdom of God and teaching the things which concern the Lord Jesus Christ with all confidence, no one forbidding him.

28:19 *a* That is, the ruling authorities   28:25 *a* NU-Text reads *your*.   28:27 *a* Isaiah 6:9, 10
28:29 *a* NU-Text omits this verse.

DEVOTIONAL PROMPTS

LUKE 1

- In verse 14, Gabriel promises Zacharias "joy and gladness, and many will rejoice" because of his son's birth. What promises of joy has the Lord given all believers?

- When Gabriel delivered his messages to Zacharias and Mary, they both questioned how his promises were possible (vv. 18, 34). When have you doubted God's ability to fulfill His plan?

- Zacharias prophesied that "we, being delivered from the hand of our enemies, might serve Him without fear" (v. 74). What does serving God without fear look like for you?

LUKE 2

• How is Jesus' birth a source of "good tidings of great joy" to you personally (v. 10)?

• Verse 40 says Jesus "became strong in spirit, filled with wisdom; and the grace of God was upon Him." How did Jesus exemplify these qualities during His human life?

• What does "being about My Father's business" mean in your life (v. 49)?

243

LUKE 3

- When you read John's description of the Messiah to come (vv. 16–18), how does it shape your understanding of Jesus' ministry?

- How do verses 21–22 reveal the Trinity to you?

- Genealogies like verses 23–38 are placed in Scripture for a reason. What does this one teach you about Jesus?

LUKE 4

- In verse 3, Satan challenged Jesus to choose physical bread over spiritual words of God. Have you ever succumbed to this temptation?

- What Scriptures have been fulfilled before you (v. 21)?

- Jesus said, "No prophet is accepted in his own country" (v. 24). Why do you think this is true?

LUKE 5

- In verses 1–11 we see Jesus calling Peter, James, and John to follow Him and "catch men." Why do you think one miracle was enough to convince them they should drop everything and obey Him?

- When Jesus healed the paralytic (vv. 17–26), which do you think benefited him most—his ability to walk or his being forgiven? Why?

- If you had been the paralytic, what would you have asked for?

LUKE 6

- Why do you think the Pharisees preferred rule-keeping to the rule of the Son of Man (vv. 1–11)?

- In verses 13–16 we see Jesus select His apostles from those who followed Him. Knowing Jesus chooses *you*, how do you feel about being His disciple?

- Jesus discussed giving to others without measure (vv. 35–36). When have you done this?

LUKE 7

- In verse 9 Jesus praised the centurion's faith. Can you express the same faith? Why or why not?

- We see Jesus restore life to a young man in verses 11–15. How does He tell you today, "I say to you, arise"?

- In verse 26 Jesus declared John the Baptist a prophet. Given John's eccentricities, would you have found that hard to believe?

253

LUKE 8

- Verses 2–3 describe the women who followed Jesus. Why was this important information for Luke to mention?

- Is there any way that you cover your "light" (v. 16)? Why?

- If you had secretly touched Jesus' hem for healing, how would you have felt when He turned and spoke to you (vv. 43–48)?

255

LUKE 9

- In verses 10–17 we witness Jesus' feeding the five thousand. How would you have felt if He had said to you, "You give them something to eat" (v. 13)?

- "Who do you say that I am?" (v. 20). How do you answer this question today?

- Do you ever catch yourself trying to gain "the whole world" (v. 25)? How do you react?

LUKE 10

- Do you ever feel like a lamb among wolves (v. 3)? If so, how?

- Is your name "written in heaven" (v. 20)? What feelings does this stir in you today?

- Have you ever acted as a good Samaritan (vv. 25–37)?

259

LUKE 11

- Do you ever pray the Lord's Prayer (vv. 2–4)? Is it useful to you?

- Are you surprised at Jesus' exhortations in verses 5–10 to seek God's aid persistently? Why or why not?

- When have you seen a divided house fall (v. 17?)

LUKE 12

- Have you experienced a time when the Holy Spirit gave you words to say in a challenging situation (vv. 11–12)? What was that like?

- What do you think Jesus means in verse 21 by implying we should be "rich toward God"?

- How hard is it to make peace with an adversary (v. 58)?

LUKE 13

- How do you think the woman who was bent over with a spirit of infirmity (v. 11) felt to have Jesus place His hands on her and heal her?

- From what would you like Jesus to heal you?

- What people group do you see as "last" today but first in the kingdom (v. 30)?

265

LUKE 14

- In verses 12–14, Jesus commands that we share with those who cannot bless us back. How do you think He will repay those who obey Him?

- When have you struggled to bear your "cross" (v. 27)?

- Describe someone you know who is a "salty" follower of Jesus (v. 34).

LUKE 15

- What do you feel when you reflect on the fact that Jesus rejoices to have you as His "sheep" (vv. 4–5)?

- Why do you think Jesus emphasized the "joy in the presence of the angels . . . over one sinner who repents" (v. 10)?

- Have you witnessed a prodigal child (vv. 11–32) return to his or her family? What happened?

LUKE 16

- Can you think of someone who was unjust in a little, and then in much (vv. 10–13)?

- Jesus said in verse 15, "God knows your hearts." How do you feel about that today?

- What things are "highly esteemed among men" yet "an abomination in the sight of God" (v. 15)?

LUKE 17

- "If he repents, forgive him" (v. 4). When have you been lavishly forgiven? When have you lavishly forgiven someone else?

- In verse 6 Jesus explains the power of faith as tiny as a mustard seed. What does that kind of faith look like to you?

- How do you express the kingdom of God within you (v. 21)?

LUKE 18

- Do you receive the kingdom of God "as a little child" (v. 17)? How so?

- When did you feel something was impossible for God—but He proved otherwise (v. 27)?

- If Jesus asked you today, "What do you want Me to do for you?" what would you answer (v. 41)?

LUKE 19

- Would you have agreed with the crowd who said Jesus "has gone to be a guest with . . . a sinner" (v. 7)?

- How can you join the disciples who, at the triumphal entry, "began to rejoice and praise God with a loud voice for all the mighty works they had seen" (v. 37)?

- How do you react to Jesus' tears (v. 41) for Jerusalem?

LUKE 20

- How is Jesus the "chief cornerstone" of your life (v. 17)?

- Today, how can you render to "Caesar" what is his and to God what is His (v. 25)?

- How do you feel that Jesus describes the dead in verse 36 as "equal to the angels and [as] sons of God"?

LUKE 21

- What does it mean for you, like the widow in verses 1–4, to give out of your poverty to God?

- How can you follow Jesus' admonition in verse 19 to possess your soul?

- Do you feel confident you will be "counted worthy . . . to stand before the Son of Man" (v. 36)? Why or why not?

281

LUKE 22

- How do you feel about Jesus' statement, "This is My body which is given for you" (v. 19)?

- How can you be like Jesus who said in verse 27, "I am among you as the One who serves"?

- Why do you think Jesus healed the servant who lost his ear (v. 51)?

287

ACTS 1

- What do you suppose Jesus' followers felt when He told them in verse 8 they would take the gospel "to the end of the earth"?

- How would you have responded to the message spoken by the two men "in white apparel" (vv. 10–11)? Who were they?

- What is the difference between a disciple and an apostle (vv. 1, 15, 26)? Which are you?

ACTS 2

- What does it mean that God "loosed the pains of death" (v. 24)?

- Have you ever made a spiritual declaration as clear as Peter's—"God has made this this Jesus . . . both Lord and Christ" (v. 36)?

- What wonders and signs have you witnessed? What was their effect on you?

ACTS 3

- What is poignant about Peter's statement to the paralyzed man in verse 6—"Silver and gold I do not have, but what I do have I give you"?

- Have you experienced "times of refreshing" from the Lord (v. 19)? If so, what was it like?

- What do you look forward to at the time of restoration of all things (v. 21)?

293

ACTS 4

- After hearing the threats of the chief priests and elders (v. 17), would you have run to hide, returned to the other disciples, or something else?

- Are you surprised by the disciples' reaction (vv. 29–30) to Peter and John's experience—praising God?

- Whom would you describe as having "great grace" (v. 33)?

295

ACTS 5

- Why did people seek to have Peter's shadow fall on them (v. 15)? What would you have done if you suffered a physical infirmity at that time?

- When have you had to choose between obeying God and obeying man (v. 29)? What was the result?

- What do you think of Gamaliel's recommendation in verses 33–39?

ACTS 6

- Do you think the apostles were correct in designating the distribution of goods to others (vv. 1–4)? Why or why not?

- Verse 7 notes that "a great many of the priests were obedient to the faith." Is this surprising? Why or why not?

- Do you know someone of whom you would say, "They were not able to resist the wisdom and the Spirit by which he spoke" (v. 10)?

ACTS 7

- When asked to respond to the charges of blasphemy, Stephen described the Hebrews' history (vv. 2–50). Why do you suppose he did that?

- Stephen spoke with great courage to his angry audience. Do you think he was wise to do so? Why or why not?

- How can you become as forgiving and rich in Spirit as Stephen was (v. 60)?

ACTS 8

- Have you experienced direction as clear as what Philip received when the angel told him to go to the desert (v. 26)?

- When have you had the opportunity to talk with someone open to the gospel?

- What do you think the Word means when it says "the Spirit of the Lord caught Philip away" (v. 39)? Would you like to have witnessed that?

303

ACTS 9

- Has the Lord surprised you as He surprised first Saul (vv. 1–9), then Ananias (vv. 10–18)?

- Was your conversion story—or that of someone you know—as dramatic as Saul's?

- Why do you think Barnabas accepted Saul's testimony (v. 27)?

ACTS 10

- Angels make several appearances in the Book of Acts. Do you think angels are as active today as they were in the years immediately following Jesus' resurrection?

- In verse 36 Peter stated clearly, "Jesus Christ—He is Lord of all." What does this truth mean to you?

- The resurrected Jesus appeared "not to all the people but to witnesses chosen before by God" (v. 41). Why do you suppose the risen Lord wasn't revealed to everyone?

ACTS 11

- Verses 1–2 say the apostles and other believers angrily confronted Peter when he returned to Jerusalem. Can you understand their objection or were they missing the point?

- Given Barnabas's character in strengthening the brethren, why do you think he sought out Saul (vv. 22–25)?

- Scripture says Barnabas was "a good man, full of the Holy Spirit and of faith" (v. 24). How would others describe you?

309

ACTS 12

- Why did Herod assign four squads of soldiers (v. 4) to guard one man?

- Have you ever had to convince people that a miracle had occurred, the way Rhoda did with the believers at Mary's house (vv. 13–15)? Were you successful?

- Has God freed you from a prison real or figurative? Thank Him today for deliverance.

ACTS 13

- What do you think made Saul and Barnabas an effective team (v. 2) for sharing the gospel?

- Verse 44 reports, "Almost the whole city came together to hear the word of God." When have you witnessed an outpouring of hunger for the Lord's Word?

- Though strife increased as the disciples preached, they "were filled with joy and with the Holy Spirit" (v. 52). Have you ever experienced joy in the midst of frightening circumstances?

ACTS 14

- Paul realized that the crippled man "had faith to be healed" (v. 9). Do you think your faith is apparent to others?

- Why are human beings so eager to worship other human beings, as the people of Lystra sought to do with Paul and Barnabas (vv. 8–18)?

- The Jews stoned Paul until they thought he was dead, but "when the disciples gathered around him, he rose up" (v. 20). What happened? Do you think he was less injured than assumed, or did God heal him?

315

ACTS 15

- Why did the Jerusalem Council opt to assign very few rules to the new Gentile believers (vv. 1–29)?

- For what reason did Paul reject taking John Mark on his journey to revisit recent believers (vv. 37–38)?

- Do you agree with Paul's reasoning, or was he being too harsh?

ACTS 16

- Visions occur frequently in Acts (for example, vv. 9–10). Do you think people still experience them, or were they a wonder for another time in history?

- When Peter was miraculously freed from prison, he went to his friends' home (12:5–17). When the jail opened for Paul and Silas, they stayed put (16:25–28). Why?

- How brave was Paul in challenging the magistrates' treatment (v. 37)? Would you have done the same thing?

ACTS 17

- Scripture reports in verses 5–8 that the envious Jews in Thessalonica stirred up opposition to the believers in the area. Have you known—or been—someone who agitates groups for personal gain?

- Why does Scripture report that Paul "reasoned" (v. 2) with the Greek Jews and Gentiles to try to persuade them to believe the gospel? Why is this approach better than simple confrontation?

- Verses 27–28 say, "He is not far from each one of us; for in Him we live and move and have our being." What do these truths mean to you?

ACTS 18

• What do you think of Gallio's response (vv. 14–16) to the angry Jews who wanted him to punish Paul?

• When Paul went to the Galatia and Phrygia region, he spent time "strengthening all the disciples" (v. 23). Is this something you do as well? How?

• Why made Apollos such a powerful and effective preacher (vv. 24–28)? Do you know anyone like that?

ACTS 19

- Why do you think God used Paul in such miraculous ways (vv. 11–12)?

- Have you witnessed a situation in which "the word of the Lord grew mightily and prevailed" (v. 20)?

- Have you ever seen someone step in to calm an angry group the way the city clerk did (vv. 21–41)? How did he or she do it?

ACTS 20

- How do you think Eutychus felt when he realized what had happened (vv. 7–12)?

- Paul determined to "finish [his] race with joy" (v. 24). How do you want to finish your race?

- Whom can you commend to God "and to the word of His grace" (v. 32)?

ACTS 21

- Has someone ever tried to dissuade you from doing what the Lord had directed you to do, as the disciples did Paul (vv. 10–12)? What happened?

- If you had been among Paul's friends, what would you have done when "all Jerusalem was in an uproar" (v. 31)?

- After being beaten and harassed by a mob, Paul thought to start preaching (vv. 37–40). Is that what you would have done in his situation?

ACTS 22

- Paul began his preaching by listing his credentials (vv. 3–16). Why was that a smart idea?

- If someone told you a story like Paul's (vv. 6–16), how would you respond?

- Was Paul wise to tell the centurion he was a Roman citizen (v. 25)? Why or why not?

ACTS 23

- When has the Lord given you an encouraging word when you most needed it, as He did Paul (v. 11)?

- Was Paul's behavior foolhardy or strategic as he faced angry mobs and agitated religious leaders (vv. 12–35)? Why?

- How would you have attempted to keep a level head during such intense opposition?

ACTS 24

- Tertullus referred to Paul as "a plague" (v. 5). When have you been—or heard someone else being—falsely accused?

- Paul responded to Tertullus's accusations by saying, "I do the more cheerfully answer for myself" (v. 10). Where does such joy come from?

- What tone of voice do you suppose Paul used in his defense (vv. 10–21)? Do his words sound desperate or whiny?

ACT 25

• How did Paul's appealing to Caesar (v. 11) play a role in furthering the gospel's spread?

• Do you see God's hand in Paul's being treated so carefully among the different leaders he faced? Would you have expected more violence?

• Again and again leaders declared that Paul had done nothing deserving death. How are echoes of Jesus' story apparent in Paul's?

ACTS 26

- Paul referred to himself as "happy" in the midst of his life being on trial (v. 2). How is it possible for a human being to feel joy in the harshest circumstances?

- Each time in the Book of Acts that Paul told the story of his conversion, the details were a bit different (vv. 12–18). Why do you think this was?

- Can you understand why Festus called Paul "mad" (v. 24)?

ACTS 27

- Paul initially predicted that the shipwreck would be a total loss of all cargo and passengers (v. 10). What changed his mind later in the chapter (v. 22)?

- Have you ever given up hope of being saved from something? What happened?

- Twice Paul urged the sailors to "take heart" (vv. 22, 25). How do you do this when circumstances are threatening?

341

ACTS 28

- First the natives of Malta called Paul a murderer (v. 4), and when he survived a viper bite, a god (v. 6). Can you understand their confusion?

- If you had Paul's healing hands (v. 8), whom would you heal? Why?

- In Rome the other prisoners were sent to jail, but Paul was allowed to "dwell by himself with the soldier who guarded him" (v. 16) Why was he afforded this privilege?